Praise for *Easy Meals to Cook with Kids*

"*Easy Meals to Cook with Kids* is one of the best cooking-with-children books I have seen yet. The information is clear, thorough, lovingly laid out - and, importantly, organized according to age level. The recipes are creative, healthful, and compelling. Congratulations on a deceptively challenging job joyfully and beautifully done! The world needs this."
   –Mollie Katzen, author of *Moosewood Cookbook* and the *Pretend Soup* children's cookbook trilogy

"In a world where many children can't name a single vegetable or fruit by sight, where families have lost the art of cooking and celebration of meals together, where the food industry markets food as "good" for us *or* "fun" for us, Julie Negrin created a magical play land of food that is both good for you AND fun for you. She introduces children to the world of health and nutrition through delighting the senses and the palate. *Easy Meals to Cook with Kids* should be used in every home and taught in every school. It will change America one bite and one smile at a time."
   –Mark Hyman, MD, New York Times best-selling author of *UltraMetabolism, UltraMind*
      and Chairman of the Institute for Functional Medicine

"*Easy Meals to Cook with Kids* is a fun, informative guide to cooking for and with your children. The recipes are tasty, nutritious and easy to follow, with age-appropriate tips for incorporating all of your budding chefs. Pick up this book and turn everyday meal preparation into a joy-filled, family-bonding experience."
   –Lisa Oz, mom and author of *US: Transforming Ourselves and the Relationships that Matter Most*

"I like *Easy Meals to Cook with Kids* so much because not only does it expose children to cooking from a very early age, but that Julie Negrin has genuine respect for children, their capabilities and all positive possibilities, born of her own in depth experience of working with children. Teaching children to cook is unquestionably important for many reasons, but to do so with joy and utter belief in children, what they can do and how they can grow, is invaluable."
   –Deborah Madison, author of *Vegetarian Cooking for Everyone*

"A love of food, a love of children, knowledge of nutrition, skill in the kitchen, passion, compassion, wisdom and insight- what a delicious recipe! That is exactly what Julie serves up in *Easy Meals to Cook with Kids*. I loved every bite - and am confident you will, too!"
   –David L. Katz, MD, MPH, FACPM, FACP, President & Founder of the Turn the Tide Foundation, Inc.

"*Easy Meals to Cook with Kids* can open up a new world for moms, dads, and kids. It shows how cooking with kids can be turned into an easy, fun, effective way to teach them everything from values to nutrition. In fact the real power of following Negrin's recipes for food is that her approach is also a recipe for becoming a closer family."
   –Dr. Brian Wansink, author of *Mindless Eating*

"Julie Negrin is part of an inspiring movement across the country reclaiming our kids' taste buds from food marketers and the fast food industry. In this tantalizing cookbook, Negrin demystifies cooking with kids, helping any parent—no matter your skill level—to safely and confidently bring kids into the kitchen. I can't wait until my daughter is old enough for us to dive into these recipes together!"
    –Anna Lappé, mom and author of *Diet for a Hot Planet: The Climate Crisis*
        at the End of Your Fork and What You Can Do About It

"The childhood obesity crises in our country must lead us to change our children's relationship to food – one of the best ways of doing that is cooking with them. *Easy Meals to Cook with Kids*, will help parents and kids cook healthy meals together and along the way help kids make life-long healthy food choices – plus, of course, have fun and eat well!"
    –Chef Ann Cooper, author of *Lunch Lessons: Changing the Way We Feed Our Children*

"*Easy Meals to Cook with Kids* is a well-thought-out book for cooking with children, with excellent advice and tips, as well as lots of very nice recipes. The whole family can enjoy this together!
    –Annemarie Colbin, Ph.D., Founder and CEO, The Natural Gourmet Institute
        for Health and Culinary Arts, NYC

"Inspiring our kids to cook is the greatest accomplishment and Julie Negrin has done it with this book. *Easy Meals to Cook with Kids* is a powerful tool to make cooking fun and healthy for the whole family. Children cooking and learning benefits everyone and future generations as well. Let's keep saving the planet one bite at a time."
    -Joy Pierson Nutritionist, owner Candle Cafe and Candle 79, Board Chair for
        New York Coalition for Healthy School Food.

"A kid- and parent-friendly, fun and flavor-packed adventure that brings families back together in the heart of the home, the kitchen, where nutrition and nourishment team up. *Easy Meals to Cook with Kids* is a delicious way to transform the health of our nation's most precious resource, our children."
    –Kathie Madonna Swift, MS RD LDN

"As someone who believes in the importance of cooking with kids, Julie shows us how much fun it can be in *Easy Meals to Cook with Kids*. And yummy, too!"
    –Bill Telepan, chef-owner Telepan Restaurant & Founder/Executive Chef, Wellness in the Schools

Easy Meals
to Cook with Kids

Healthy, Family-Friendly Recipes
from Around the World

By Julie Negrin, M.S., C.N.

AuthorHouse™
1663 Liberty Drive
Bloomington, IN 47403
www.authorhouse.com
Phone: 1-800-839-8640

First published by AuthorHouse 9/20/2010

ISBN: 978-1-4520-8067-3 (sc)

Printed in the United States of America

This book is printed on acid-free paper.

authorHOUSE®

For my nieces and nephews

Josh, Gabi, Daniel, Meital, Jonah, and Yaakov

Acknowledgments

Easy Meals to Cook with Kids is a homegrown book that would not exist without the support, guidance, and encouragement of some extraordinary people.

I want to give a huge shout-out to my talented designer, Josh Tuininga, who patiently tolerated my questions, requests, and last-minute changes. I feel extremely fortunate that he is my Creative Director.

My early days in the kitchen (with my brother).

The JCC in Manhattan enabled me to grow as an educator and writer. Two JCC colleagues in particular, Karen Sander and Yitzi Zablocki, helped pave the way for the writing of this book. I'm especially thankful to the parents of my JCC students who persuaded me to create this book so that other families could enjoy my recipes.

At the JCC in Manhattan, I worked with an incredible team of chef instructors who continue to inspire me: Lauren Braun Costello, David Glickman, John Scoff, Jennifer Clair, Adeena Sussman, Myra Kornfeld, Jacob Pine, Michelle Brenn-White, Stefania Patinella, Joan Richter, Jennifer Abadi, Sherri Maxman, Emily Klein, and Michelle Spiegel. I'm grateful that I had two remarkable teachers, Maggie Ward and Jacquie Grinberg, to collaborate with when developing the curriculum for the JCC kids' program.

I want to acknowledge my writing teachers and classmates in New York City who pushed me to find my writing voice. Marci Alboher deserves a special thank you for encouraging me to write this book and for continuing to support my writing endeavors.

More heartfelt thanks to:

- Laura Mozes and Anne Grossman for pulling together the photo shoot for the book cover in a mere four days.

- Anne's son, Max Freund (the little boy on the cover), for being the best child model ever.

- Megan Rose Stolber, dear friend for the past thirty years and mother of three children, for her advice on everything from the book title to the cooking tips in each recipe.

- My other lifelong friends, Carin Brody, Elana Patel, and Aimee Rivkin, for talking me through the rough moments and always making me laugh.

- Erin Olivo, Adeena Sussman, and Rob Roberts for always believing in me, my work, and this project.

- My Bastyr University and HealthCorps students and colleagues for their encouragement.

- My Auntie Janet and Uncle Larry Jassen for being a supportive second set of parents and my maternal grandparents, Annabelle and Albert Benezra for sharing their love of food and cooking with me.

- My siblings and cousins, Andy, Rick, Laura, Tony, Danny, Alex, and Sonya (and their spouses, Galit, Jodi, Jason, Shiri, Leslie, and Etan), who manage to make me feel loved and supported even when they are teasing me – which is most of the time.

- My terrific recipe testers and manuscript editors who kindly volunteered their time in the kitchen and on the computer.

- My niece and nephew, Gabi and Josh Negrin, who helped dream up the book title.

- The rest of my friends and family, who deserve sainthood for putting up with my near obsession with completing this book. Without them, I would not have left my computer or the kitchen for months.

Nobody deserves a bigger thank you than my phenomenal parents, Saralyn and Marvin Negrin. No matter how outrageous my dreams, they are always right next to me cheering me on.

Recipe Testers

Anne Grossman
Hillary Milken
Anne Curtis
Alyssa Brin
Elyse Wagner
Carin Brody
Alex Richardson
Jennifer Hoverson
Marley Peale
Hayley Gillespie
Sarah Silins
Rebekah Langford

Recipe Editors

Alyssa Brin
Anne Curtis
Merav Levkowitz
Maggie Ward
Jacquie Grinberg
Christina Lee
Israel Lopez Alderete

Manuscript Editors

Carole Glickfeld, www.caroleglickfeld.com
Lisa Tuininga, www.the-medium.net
Stephanie Gailing
Alex Jassen
Gila Schwarzschild
Scott Taylor, www.bluerobot.net

Photography

Cover photo by Laura Mozes,
   www.lauramozes.com
Head shot on back cover by Jon Wasserman,
   www.jonwassermanphotography.com
Photo editing by Theo Morrison,
   www.theomorrison.com
Food photography by Julie Negrin
   (three photos by Trevor Frydenlund)

Design

Josh Tuininga, www.the-medium.net

Recipe Development

All recipes developed by Julie Negrin
unless stated otherwise.

My Story

"If help and salvation are to come, they can only come from the children, for the children are the makers of men." –Maria Montessori

I've been taking care of kids since I was six years old. I'm the second born of four kids. My four cousins, all younger than I am, lived across the street and were (and still are) like siblings. When I was nine years old, I was an expert at heating a bottle with a crying baby on my hip. By the time I was eleven, I happily helped feed, diaper, bathe, and care for six little ones. We ran back and forth between each other's houses, built forts, played ball, held barbeques in the back yard, celebrated birthdays together, and regularly shared long, boisterous meals with our grandparents and extended family. We are Sephardic Jews, after all, which means we take our meals very seriously. (Sephardic Jews originally hailed from Spain, were expelled during the Inquisition, and settled all over the world. My great-grandparents, Papu and Nona, came from Greece and Turkey and settled in Seattle at the turn of the century.) I loved helping my mom and aunt in the kitchen as much as I adored taking care of the kids. On every holiday, and even on minor occasions, our table was crammed with family, friends, neighbors, and delicious home-cooking. In my world, family is food and food is family.

From left to right: My great-grandparents, Pearl and Leon Benezra, and my maternal grandpa, Albert Benezra selling produce at their stand at Pike Place Market in Seattle, WA (c. 1940's).

Even with all this exposure to excellent homemade meals, I was a picky eater. I ate very few foods but nobody paid much attention. Separate meals were not prepared for me and no one begged me to eat. The adults in my life were much too busy consuming their own meals, with gusto. Inadvertently, they handled my pickiness exactly as they should have: They served well-balanced meals, they modeled good eating habits, and they didn't make a big deal out of it or serve me something different from everyone else.

As often happens, my taste buds eventually matured as a teen. I discovered salads and other nutritious foods after noticing that I performed better at soccer practice if I ate a wholesome lunch. Like many others in my family, though, I started suffering from stomach problems. Within weeks of my initial symptoms, I was hospitalized.

I was diagnosed with Ulcerative Colitis (UC), an inflammatory bowel disease. It was a very severe case, affecting my entire colon, which was very inflamed. The only drug I responded to was prednisone, a steroid medication with awful side effects. I assumed that diet would influence a digestive disease but was told that it didn't matter what I ate or drank because I would be sick for the rest of my life. I was seventeen years old.

I never pictured myself staying sick. Regrettably, I was too young and uninformed to know how to transform my vision of a healthier body into a reality. So, I landed in the hospital again on my twentieth birthday. Both my parents have cousins who are naturopathic doctors and suggested that I try natural remedies. I had nothing to lose at that point – except for my colon, which I refused to allow the doctors to surgically remove despite their urging.

Though the information I found regarding diet and stomach problems was limited, I researched other treatment options, conducted self-experiments with food, and set up appointments with alternative medical practitioners. Over the next few years, I flitted between taking care of myself and acting like a typical college student.

During a particularly rough time, when I was very ill, a book caught my eye because of its title: *The Self-Healing Cookbook*, by Kristina Turner. The author suggested that a macrobiotic diet, based on mostly cooked vegetables, grains, beans, and sea vegetables could be therapeutic. While doctors never mentioned anything about healing my colon, this book gave me hope that changing my diet could improve my health. Even though I was quite weak at the time, I somehow found the energy to cook Turner's recipes. Every time I ate them, I not only felt stronger, I felt nourished – beyond just a physical level. My family watched the color come back to my cheeks as I happily bustled around the kitchen.

After six years of an intense regimen that included acupuncture, Chinese herbs, high-quality supplements, stress management, and an improved diet, I went into remission (medication- and symptom-free). At this writing, I have been doing well for over twelve years (after being sick for nearly ten). Today, I still have a sensitive stomach and work hard for my health, but overall, I'm doing well. I feel very lucky that I can enjoy activities that used to be next to impossible for me: traveling, exercising, working hard, and most of all – eating!

Cooking not only led to my recovery, it inspired a career. Changing my diet influenced how the rest of my family approached food and made me realize that one person, no matter how old, can motivate his or her relatives to modify their eating habits. This is why I became a nutritionist and kids' cooking teacher. It's extremely powerful to teach young people how to cook – it can start a ripple effect with far-reaching impact.

Sunday night dinner at the Negrin house

Kids are much more open to nutritious foods than we give them credit for and they often want to eat healthier. It breaks my heart to see so many young children who are sick or on the road to becoming sick. It's crucial that we give them the tools to prepare wholesome meals from scratch. I truly believe that it's possible for this country to cook its way back to better health. Once children are empowered to feed themselves, they have the opportunity to show their families, classmates, teachers, communities, and future generations, that the key to good health starts in the kitchen.

It's my hope that this book will open more than just kitchen doors – I hope that it inspires children to explore food on many levels. More than anything, though, I want kids to discover a love of cooking that lasts a lifetime.

Keep cookin',

Julie

Contents

Introduction

"While we try to teach our children all about life, our children teach us what life is all about." –Angela Schwindt

Welcome to *Easy Meals to Cook with Kids*! I'm thrilled to share the most popular recipes from my cooking classes based on feedback from hundreds of kids and their parents.

Because of my background in both nutrition and cooking, I like teaching my students how to prepare dishes that are healthy *and* delicious. When I first started cooking with children over twelve years ago, I wanted to make something other than sugary baked goods with them. I researched other cultures' cuisines for fun recipes that incorporate plenty of plant-based ingredients. Some parents were unsure that their picky eaters would enjoy my classes, but I quickly discovered that kids are much more receptive to new foods if they are involved in the meal preparation. My students, as young as two years old, would gobble up all kinds of "grown up" foods including brown rice, sautéed mushrooms, tofu, kidney beans, and caramelized onions!

I've had the pleasure of watching many of my students transform into talented little chefs. Their love of cooking inspired *Easy Meals to Cook with Kids*. Each recipe in this book, therefore, includes age-appropriate kitchen tasks for children ages two years old and older so that any child can discover his or her own "inner chef." Although cooking homemade meals with children can sound daunting to tired parents, this book is designed specifically for busy families. It offers lots of cooking tips and simple, nutritious recipes that can be made in bulk and refrigerated or frozen for last-minute meals.

Not cooking with your own kids? As an auntie of six nieces and nephews, I know there are many dedicated aunts, uncles, grandparents, babysitters, and family friends who are taking time out of their busy lives to cook with children, but for simplicity's sake, I use the phrase "you and your kids" throughout the book.

In this cookbook, you'll find:

- Recipes that have been thoroughly tested and carefully written so that novice cooks and children can confidently follow the instructions.

- Inexpensive ingredients that can be found in most grocery stores (and a few ingredients that may be purchased at a health food store).

- Dishes made with "real" foods – no preservatives, additives, or trans-fats.

- Mostly vegetarian recipes that are nut-free and can be made kosher.

- Gluten- and dairy-free recipes that are designated with these icons:

Chapter 1

Why Cook with Kids?

Given that parents feel pressured to do so much for their children, "cooking a meal together" often means passing out cheese and crackers in the car. However, cooking isn't as time-consuming as you might think. One study showed that people who cook from scratch spend only a few minutes longer in the kitchen than those who prepare meals from partially prepared, packaged foods. Once your kids get the hang of helping out in the kitchen, the preparation time will be even shorter!

Every child is an artist. The problem is to remain an artist once they grow up.

Pablo Picasso

There are many benefits of including children in the meal preparation:

Exposure to scratch cooking helps kids develop a mature palate and a taste for fresh, wholesome ingredients. The earlier kids become accustomed to nutritious foods, the less likely they will acquire a taste for processed foods.

Kids are much more likely to eat what they make. Is there anything more fun than eating your art project? Cooking creates a sense of ownership. When kids help in the kitchen, there are fewer meal-time battles and more willingness to try new foods.

Meals prepared from scratch usually contain more nutrients and fewer calories, chemicals, and sweeteners than pre-packaged foods and restaurant meals.

Cooking together provides a natural way to discuss nutrition and the impact that food choices have on the environment. The more educated children are about food, the more likely they will appreciate your suggestions to eat something healthy.

The earlier they learn how to cook, the sooner they will learn an essential life skill. It's hard to imagine that teaching a three year old how to break an egg could result in a culinary protégé, but kids often become quite talented in the kitchen. This makes the messy floors worth it down the road when they start to cook for you.

Spending time in the kitchen gives them confidence. Kids thrive on feeling accomplished. Cooking is an ideal way to boost self-worth and teach responsibility. There is nothing cuter than watching children proudly serving their food to others.

Preparing meals together means quality time as a family. Cooking with children when they are young offers an opportunity to communicate with them on a regular basis. Your time chatting and cooking in the kitchen together becomes even more important as they reach the adolescent and teenage years.

What else do they learn? Science, language, counting, fractions, budgeting, weighing, sequencing, measuring, problem-solving, sharing, fine motor skills, reading, and learning about other cultures – to name just a few important things!

Meital helping in the garden

Chapter 2

How to Cook with Kids

Many people are surprised that I encourage such young children to work in the kitchen. It's easy to forget that kids pick up new skills very quickly and are naturally creative – which makes them ideal chef assistants. They often don't mind doing things that adults would find annoying like picking leaves off of fresh herbs and squeezing every last drop out of a lemon. If you're worried about your little ones getting in the way, set up a "work station" for them at the dinner table so you can freely bustle around the kitchen.

You can learn many things from children.
How much patience you have, for instance.

Franklin P. Jones

Getting Started

It's important that your first cooking experience with children is a positive one, so pick a time when everyone is relaxed and well-fed – perhaps a Saturday brunch or a Sunday night dinner.

Start with something familiar. When introducing the concept of cooking to kids, it's important to start with one of their favorite dishes so that they equate cooking with something they already enjoy. Once they get the hang of it and trust the process, you can graduate to more unusual dishes.

Find assistants. Invite Grandma over or keep your sitter for an extra hour. It'll be more fun for everyone if there is someone else to help oversee the project and clean up.

Accept that it will get messy. Plan on some mess and you'll feel less stressed. Kids are great cleaner-uppers so ask them to pitch in. Many kids, as young as 2 years old, love using a sponge and do a surprisingly good job of wiping up.

Give specific instructions. Kids think very literally, so be extremely clear with them. Years ago, I asked my students to peel carrots and turned around. When I looked again, just minutes later, they had peeled the entire carrot down. (From this experience, I realized it was a safe way for them to "grate" the carrot and continued using that method to prep carrots.)

Roll with the punches. If something goes wrong, just laugh. It's a good opportunity to teach children how to shrug off mistakes and learn from their blunders. Best of all, that "mistake" could end up being a new recipe idea for family dinners!

Respect their wishes. If they aren't interested in cooking, it's okay. The non-cooks can still contribute to the meal in other ways such as: washing produce, cleaning off cans, setting the table, folding napkins, deciding which platters to use, garnishing the dishes, clearing the table, and tasting each dish to determine if it needs additional seasoning.

Praise their efforts. They adore making food for family members so give them lots of compliments when they complete a task well – genuine, well-deserved praise builds self-worth and confidence.

Caveat

The suggestions in this book regarding which tasks are appropriate for children are just general guidelines. The maturity and abilities of each child should be assessed by the supervising adult.

Hygiene and Safety

Here are some suggestions on how to keep the kitchen clean and safe for your mini chefs.

Hand-washing. I'm extremely strict about hand-washing: all of my students, even the toddlers, must hit the sink before working with food. I show them how to use warm water and soap, scrub well, and dry their hands in order to prevent spreading germs. The ideal amount of time for hand-washing is at least 20 seconds. While hand sanitizers are good for when you're in a pinch in public, it's best to teach children to wash their hands in the sink when they are cooking.

Using knives. Small children, as young as two years old, can use plastic knives, metal butter knives, and lettuce cutters with close supervision. They are sharp enough to chop most produce (except vegetables such as onions, carrots, and potatoes) but dull enough that they can't cause any serious accidents. It's often the grater and peeler that are the most dangerous. Keep a close watch on little fingers when they use those tools!

Hot equipment and electrical appliances. I don't allow children to open the oven or work at the stove by themselves unless they are 10 or older and/or extremely mature. I also don't allow children under the age of 10 to work with electrical appliances unless an adult is overseeing the project. All electrical appliances should stay unplugged unless in use.

In case of emergencies. It's a good idea to store a fire extinguisher in a spot that older children can reach and teach them how to use it. I recommend reminding kids what to do if there is a fire: they should not throw water on it but, rather, they should find an adult who can cut off its oxygen supply (like putting a lid on a pot or keeping the oven shut). All children should be taught how to call 9-1-1 in case of an emergency.

Cross-contamination

It's important to note that any time you are working with meat, poultry or fish, you should use a clean plastic or glass cutting board (versus wood which is porous and can absorb bacteria).

You must never cut animal products and then use the same knife or cutting board to cut fruits or vegetables. Instead, the knife and board should be thoroughly cleaned with hot soapy water (or in a dishwasher) and air dried. Kids should also be reminded to wash their hands thoroughly after working with meat, poultry, fish, or eggs.

Kitchen Tasks for Different Age Groups

When working with kids in the kitchen, it's hard to strike a balance between being too laid-back and too involved, especially if they are struggling with a task. If they are having a hard time, I recommend waiting a minute before stepping in to help. Offer verbal suggestions first, and if that doesn't work, put your hand over theirs and do the task together. That way, they can learn a new motion or skill. It's important to help children feel a sense of ownership over a dish – while also making sure that it turns out edible so that they feel successful. Allowing children to find their own way through the cooking process is a rewarding experience for both adult and child.

Tasks for Kids

For each recipe, I divided the instructions into five age categories: 2 and up; 4 and up; 6 and up; 8 and up; and one for only "Adults." I allow kids 10 and up to do tasks designated for "Adults" by themselves so long as there is an adult nearby.

The following are suggested tasks for each age group. Of course, maturity and dexterity differ in each child. It's up to you to determine what's appropriate for your child.

2-3 year olds and up

Most toddlers enjoy helping in the kitchen. They are very tactile and love the concept of eating their art project. This age group, however, needs very close adult supervision since their dexterity and motor skills are still developing. Keep in mind, though, that toddlers are sponges and usually pick up skills very quickly, so don't underestimate their abilities! Just give them lots of counter space and big bowls to work with because they have trouble doing things in small spaces.

This age group can do the following tasks with minimal assistance: Squeezing lemons or limes, using a plastic juicer, washing produce in the sink, drying produce in a salad spinner; picking fresh herb leaves off stems, ripping them into small pieces; tearing up lettuce, sprinkling dried herbs and salt, using a pepper grinder, kneading dough, scooping potatoes or yams out of the skins, brushing (or "painting") oil with a pastry brush, using the rolling pin for dough or puff pastry, whisking together vinaigrettes, squeezing water out of thawed spinach, stirring, and mashing.

They will need close supervision to: Grate, peel, chop vegetables and herbs with a knife, and break eggs.

This age group can master basic tasks like breaking eggs and kneading dough:

Breaking an Egg – Let kids practice in a large, sturdy bowl with some paper towels nearby for messes:

Have them hold the egg with their dominant hand and hold the side of the bowl very securely with the other hand. Have them gently tap the center of the egg on the edge of the bowl until there is a small crack. Over the bowl, have them hold the egg so that the cracked side is facing down and both of their thumbs are over the hole. Then, instruct them to carefully pull the egg apart so that the egg slides into the bowl.

Kneading dough – Here are three steps that I use to teach small children (and grown-ups) how to knead dough. This is an oversimplified explanation for a fast-moving technique, but it's helpful for kids to have a step-by-step method that they can repeat to themselves during the task. Once the dough is in a ball, have them Fold, Press, Turn.

1) **Fold** over the top half of the dough
2) **Press** with the heels of their palms
3) **Turn** the dough halfway around the surface

   Keep repeating this process for 3-5 minutes.

4-5 year olds and up

In this age group, there is a lot of variability in motor skills, independence, and the ability to focus, which means that some kids will continue doing the 2-3 year-old tasks, and others will feel ready to move on to the 6-7 year-old tasks.

6-7 year olds and up

This age group usually has developed fine motor skills so they can take on more detailed work, like using measuring spoons and forming evenly sized patties. They may still need reminders to watch their fingers during grating and peeling.

They also excel at: Dicing and mincing vegetables, grating cheese; peeling raw potatoes, ginger, mangoes and other fruits and vegetables; slicing and scooping out avocados, greasing pans, using a microplane zester, de-seeding tomatoes and roasted peppers, draining and slicing tofu, rinsing grains and beans, forming cookies and patties, pouring liquids into small containers, and garnishing (or "decorating") dishes.

8-9 year olds and up

There is a wide range of skills in this age group. Some 8 year olds are not mature enough to work at the stove. Others have the focus and diligence of an adult. You'll have to decide if they should continue with the 6-7 year old tasks or if they are responsible enough to do more.

This group can take on more sophisticated tasks such as: Using a pizza cutter and can opener, scooping batter into muffin cups, scraping down the (unplugged) electric mixer bowl and food processor bowl, putting away leftovers, pounding chicken, proofing yeast, skewering food, slicing bread, and chopping hot chili peppers (latex gloves are a good idea!).

10-12 year olds and up

This age group can usually work independently in the kitchen. Before letting them do grown-up tasks on their own, they should have close adult supervision to assess whether they can follow basic rules such as:

Josh and his brother, Daniel making calzones together.

- Keeping pan handles tucked into the stove

- Unplugging electrical appliances as soon as they are done using them

- Covering both hands in large oven mitts when removing something from the oven

- Safely using a chef's knife and carrying it correctly (pointed down at the floor)

- Turning the oven and stove off when they are done using them

Once they pass a few of these "tests," they can move onto basic tasks at the stove (stirring, making eggs) and oven, or using a chef's knife, without close adult supervision. However, I recommend that there still be an adult in the house in case of emergency.

Chapter 3

Shopping and Stocking Ingredients

Deciding which ingredients to buy for one simple dish isn't always a straight-forward process. In order to make your cooking experiences truly "easy," it's helpful to become proficient at grocery shopping and stocking the pantry.

Children are our most valuable natural resource.

Herbert Hoover

Finding the Best Ingredients

The more we cook with high-quality "real foods," the more refined our palates will become. Even if you have budget constraints or can't find certain products, keep in mind that a homemade meal made with love is always superior to anything else.

The "Gold Standard." In an ideal world, we'd be growing our own food, but that's not feasible for many of us! The next best thing is finding local, organic produce and pasture-raised, organic animal products. Some small farmers can't afford third-party organic certification but still use sustainable farming methods. Research online for information about specific brands or speak with farmers and ranchers at a farmer's market. Trustworthy vendors freely give information and will often invite you to their farm.

Contains no preservatives, additives, or trans fats – all recipes are made with wholesome, natural foods!

Focus on "clean" foods that are also "whole." When I say "clean," I mean products without pesticides, hormones, antibiotics, and other chemicals. "Whole" foods contain only one ingredient – themselves (e.g., brown rice, oats, beans, nuts, seeds, vegetables, fruit, chicken, fish).

Buy in season. Seasonal produce is cheaper and of better quality when it's been picked recently – and preferably, not shipped very far. Encourage your kids to conduct blind "taste tests" between a locally grown tomato versus a tomato from far away. The more interactive the food activity, the more likely kids will remember the lesson they've learned.

Get creative. Your local supermarket often has hidden gems. Pepper the staff with questions – the produce manager, fishmonger, and other store employees are often very knowledgeable. Request pasture-raised meat and poultry that does not contain antibiotics or hormones. Many stores appreciate knowing what their customers wish to buy. If it's hard to locate decent, seasonal produce, try frozen products. They offer a good source of nutrients since they are usually "flash-frozen" right after being picked.

Stock up on flavor-enhancing ingredients. Explore your local supermarkets for items such as vinegars, oils, spices, tomato products, olives, capers, artichokes, mustards, dried peppers, dried mushrooms, and ethnic ingredients. They can transform a basic meal into a delectable, flavorful feast for very little money.

Minimize the use of packaged foods – especially those that boast how "natural" and "healthy" they are. The healthiest items typically don't have million-dollar marketing campaigns declaring how good they are for you (e.g., broccoli, lentils). Read food labels carefully! If you can't pronounce what's in it, then it's usually not worth eating.

Limit "kiddie" foods. While kids deserve a treat once in a while in order to not feel deprived, most "kiddie" foods are processed and expensive. Instead, offer treats like homemade cookies or high-quality chocolate.

Educate your kids. Food marketers spend millions of dollars to encourage kids to "nag" their parents to buy their products. Initiate discussions with your kids about food products being advertised on television, where food comes from, and what their growing bodies need. The more educated they are about food and health, the more likely they will make the right choices.

Stocking Your Kitchen

Keeping your kitchen organized and well-stocked makes it much easier to cook healthy meals at home.

Create a grocery list. Create your own ingredient list template in an Excel spreadsheet or find one online. Or, go the low-tech route and simply leave a piece of paper in the same spot in the kitchen so that each family member can add to the list. This will save you time and money because you'll be more likely to buy only what you need.

Organize your pantry and refrigerator. Move old products to the front to be used up first, and store products in sealed containers to keep them fresh longer. Clean out your pantry as often as possible so that it doesn't get overstuffed with unused items which can be donated to a food bank.

How Do You Know What's In Season?

It depends on where you live and which crops are grown in your area but here is a very general chart of produce by season.

For more detailed information, visit www.nrdc.org/health/foodmiles.

Spring: asparagus, artichokes, radishes, spring onions, leeks, peas, garlic, scallions, and beets

Summer: berries, cherries, corn, tomatoes, carrots, peas, beans, beets, okra, summer squash, zucchini, eggplant, peppers, fennel, broccoli rabe, and many fruits

Fall: pumpkins, broccoli, pomegranates, cauliflower, mushrooms, potatoes, celery, apples, pears, mushrooms, and Brussels sprouts

Winter: leafy greens, leeks, carrots, and root vegetables such as sweet potato, yam, winter squash, turnips, celeriac, rutabaga, and parsnips

Enlist the kids to systematize the pantry and establish shelf space for each category:

Grains and pastas: rice, quinoa, soba noodles, couscous, pasta

Cereals and crackers: boxed cereal, oatmeal, crackers, popcorn

Cans and jars: black, white, and kidney beans; chickpeas, lentils, tomato products, corn, artichokes, olives, anchovies, capers

Bottles and boxes: vinegars, vegetable/chicken stock, oils

Spices and dried goods: spices, sesame and sunflower seeds, dried fruit, teas

Refrigerated items: produce, dairy products, whole-grain bread, miso, tamari, mirin, maple syrup, mustards, crushed garlic, Worcestershire sauce, tahini, brown rice syrup

Freezer items: meat/poultry/fish, frozen produce, nuts (to preserve freshness), puff pastry

Spices

Spices can provide a dash of culinary magic to any dish. However, for this cookbook, I toned down strong flavors to make the recipes kid-friendly.

If some members of your family prefer a little "kick," they can add the following to their own serving: crushed red pepper, cayenne, chili pepper, cumin, curry powder, horseradish, fresh ginger, wasabi, Tabasco, ground chipotle, chiplote peppers in adobe sauce, dried chili peppers, chili paste, or Sriracha sauce (a spicy, Asian red sauce).

Unique Ingredients

In order to minimize your trips to the grocery store, most of the ingredients in this book can be found at your local supermarket. Because the recipes are ethnic and healthy, however, there are a few products that you may need to purchase at a health food store. Most of them are non-perishable and relatively inexpensive so you shouldn't have to buy them often. Many supermarket chains now carry these products – check there first: Tofu, brown rice, rice vinegar, tahini, brown rice syrup, mirin (sweet rice wine), tamari (wheat-free soy sauce), toasted sesame oil, miso, quinoa, all-natural maple syrup, pita pockets, dumpling wrappers, Mexican cheese, masa harina (corn flour), corn tortillas, and trans-fat-free puff pastry.

Main Ingredients

Buying quality ingredients can be costly, so start small and upgrade one or two products at a time.

Oils: Some oils are better than others. Reputable companies will often label how the oil was extracted and bottle it in dark glass rather than clear plastic. If possible, try to buy organic oils – they are more expensive but worth it. Oil should be stored in a tightly sealed container in a cool, dark cupboard away from heat. When cooking with oil, make sure it's hot before adding food! To determine if the oil is ready, add a small piece of food to the pan. If it sizzles, then it's ready. However, if the oil starts to smoke, then you've gone above the "smoke point" and burned it.

Wipe out the pan and start over. You can find the smoke points for individual oils on the Internet but for general purposes, use canola oil, sunflower oil, and ghee for high-heat methods like pan-frying, and save olive oil, butter, and coconut oil for low-heat cooking like sautéing.

Butter: Butter is a "real" food that our bodies know how to process and digest, which makes it superior to fake butter products and margarines that contain hydrogenated oils (which are the harmful trans-fats). With that said, butter is a saturated fat and eating too much of it has been linked to many chronic diseases; use it sparingly. Buy the unsalted version so that you can control the sodium content of each dish. Like most animal products, it's best to buy an organic brand to avoid ingesting unnecessary chemicals. For families that can't tolerate dairy products, look for non-hydrogenated margarine products.

Salt & Pepper: Salt gets a bad rap even though the real culprit is the large quantities of refined sodium in processed and fast foods. The more meals we cook at home, the less likely we'll exceed our sodium requirements. Look for kosher salt or a high quality sea salt, which contains important minerals. Both products are usually less processed than regular table salt. I also recommend investing in a pepper grinder – most kids love using one, and freshly ground pepper tastes much better than pre-ground pepper.

In a Pinch

When preparing a dish entirely from scratch just isn't possible, try to use store-bought products that don't contain lots of additives, preservatives, or added sugars. Rather than using lemon juice concentrate, find a bottle of the fresh, organic kind at the health food store. Or, keep jarred crushed garlic in the refrigerator – kids often prefer it because it's sweeter and less pungent than fresh garlic.

Sugar: Our bodies can tolerate very small amounts of sugar, yet Americans eat far too much of it these days. The majority of our intake is low-quality, man-made sugars (like high fructose corn syrup) found in beverages, fast foods, and processed products. We should consume sugar infrequently and, ideally, in homemade baked goods so that we know exactly what we are eating. While refined white sugar is preferable to artificial sweeteners (which children should not ingest), lots of natural sweeteners are fun to experiment with in the kitchen, including mirin, molasses, honey, maple syrup, brown rice syrup, and date sugar. If your family needs a more gradual shift toward natural sweeteners, check out brands such as Sucanat, Rapadura, and Florida Crystals.

Dairy: Most dairy products in the United States (U.S.) contain hormones and antibiotics unless they are organic or otherwise labeled. For many families, deciding to eat or abstain from dairy is a personal decision. If you do purchase dairy products for your children (especially milk), I recommend buying organic brands from reputable companies. With food allergies on the rise, it's a good idea to pay close attention to whether your children have trouble digesting milk products.

Soy: Soy foods are a great source of protein. However, the majority of soy crops grown in the U.S. are grown with seeds with genetically modified organisms (GMOs). The only way to avoid GMOs is to buy organic brands. Ideally, we should stick to "whole food" soy products like edamame, miso, tamari, tofu, and tempeh, and limit processed products that contain non-organic soy derivatives. You must read food labels carefully in order to avoid GMO soy.

Meat/Poultry/Eggs: I recommend the same advice for meat, poultry, and eggs as I do for milk – avoid the chemicals. Although it can be costly and hard to find in your area, try to buy from ranchers whose animals are grass-fed, treated humanely, have spent the majority of their lives outside, and have not been given antibiotics or hormones. Keep in mind that "free-range," "cage-free," "grass-fed," and other claims on the label may not reflect what's really happening on the farms, so it's best to do your own research. For more information on food labels, check the United States Department of Agriculture (USDA) website at www.usda.gov or call the USDA Meat and Poultry Hotline at 1-888-MPHotline.

Fish: Figuring out which kind of fish is safe to buy can be quite complicated these days. We have to worry about potential toxins as well as environmental concerns like overfishing and non-sustainable fishing methods. For information on mercury, check the Environmental Protection Agency website at www.epa.gov/mercury or the Natural Resources Defense Council website at www.nrdc.org. If you want to learn how to purchase sustainable fish, you can print off the latest (free) seafood pocket guide on the Monterey Bay Aquarium website at www.montereybayaquarium.org.

Produce/Grains: There are a lot of variables to consider when buying produce. If you can't find or afford local, organic produce, try to find fruits and vegetables from your region that are as "clean" as possible. And limit produce that was brought in from other countries since it's usually not environmentally friendly. If you're worried about how many pesticides your family is exposed to, check the Environmental Working Group's (EWG) website, www.ewg.org for a list of the most highly sprayed fruits and vegetables (called "The Dirty Dozen") and the least sprayed (called the "The Clean 15"). Try to purchase whole grains like brown rice, quinoa, and oats rather than processed products that contain enriched flour, sugar, and other additives.

Since purchasing local and organic produce at the store can be expensive, try joining a Community Supported Agriculture (CSA) program. As a CSA member, you'll support farmers in your region and receive weekly or bi-monthly boxes of produce, sometimes delivered right to your doorstep! Check out www.localharvest.org to find a CSA in your area.

Check out my website, www.julienegrin.com, for additional resources and information.

Chapter 4

Essential Kitchen Equipment

Owning the right kitchen equipment guarantees a much smoother cooking experience. It's unnecessary to buy a bunch of fancy gadgets, but it is important to have the basics. I prioritized the following lists to help you determine which tools your family needs. Before you start shopping, I recommend doing some research, because there are often discount stores, department store sales, and restaurant suppliers that sell equipment at a fraction of the retail price.

A child can ask questions that a wise man cannot answer.

Author Unknown

Essential Equipment

Chef's knife. Rather than spend your money on a knife set, you're better off investing in a quality chef's knife that will last many years. The average size is an 8-inch knife. Wash it by hand and store it carefully in a knife sheath or in its own compartment in a kitchen drawer.

Paring knife and serrated knife. Also worth purchasing are a paring knife (for peeling and other intricate work) and a serrated knife (for slicing bread and tomatoes).

Cutting boards. If you're only going to buy one, it should be plastic, since you can use it for all products including meat, poultry, and fish.

Baking sheet. It's easier to cook in bulk when you own at least two, if not more, baking sheets with edges (otherwise known as jellyroll pans) that are 12½-inch by 17½-inch. Stainless steel pans last longer than non-stick, which chip easily and need to be replaced often.

Mixing bowls. A set of stainless steel mixing bowls that includes small to large sizes is essential. You can also buy glass ones but they are heavier and harder for kids to maneuver.

Measuring tools. Buy at least two sets of measuring spoons so that when one set inevitably goes missing, you have a back-up. It's also a good idea to own at least two sets of dry measuring cups and two liquid measuring cups (the Pyrex glass ones are a good choice) so that you don't have to be cleaning constantly while you are cooking with your kids.

Knife Skills

I highly recommend taking a knife skills class even if you've been cooking for years. Learning how to properly use a chef's knife will cut down on your prep time and improve your overall cooking because evenly cut vegetables are less likely to be undercooked or burned.

Common cutting terms:

Mince is when you chop food into very small pieces, commonly used for garlic.

Dice refers to a perfect cube, typically between ¼-inch and ¾-inch.

Chop is when you cut food into medium-sized pieces when uniformity is not necessary.

Strainer/Colander. I recommend owning a fine mesh strainer for small grains and other tiny ingredients and a metal colander with large holes for draining pasta.

Oven thermometer. Many ovens are not well-calibrated – even new ones may be off by quite a few degrees. Your best bet is to purchase an inexpensive oven thermometer and keep it inside your oven, especially when you bake.

Timers. There are great digital ones on the market. Find one you like and buy at least two (in different colors, if possible!) for when you're cooking multiple dishes.

Baking pans. Depending on how much your family bakes, the bare minimum bakeware would be one 9-inch by 13-inch pan, one 8-inch by 8-inch pan, and two standard 12-cup muffin tins. Pie dishes, bread pans, and round cake pans are also useful.

Pans. Feel free to purchase more pans but the "must haves" are: an 8-inch omelet pan, an 8-inch skillet, a 10-inch or 12-inch sauté pan (one with edges), a 2-quart saucepan, a 4- or 6-quart saucepan, and an 8-quart stock pot (or Dutch oven). Try to buy a decent brand for your "must haves" and make sure the larger pots have heavy bottoms so that your soups and sauces don't burn.

Storage Containers. Quality containers are essential for families who want to store leftovers. I recommend containers (and lunch boxes) that do not contain toxins such as lead or Bisphenol-A (BPA), which is found in many plastic products and may cause health problems. Check online for all-natural products.

Inexpensive, Useful Tools (That Are Fun for Kids)

Blender, electric hand mixer, steamer basket, plastic juicer, tongs, pizza cutter, U-shaped peeler, box cheese grater, whisk, rolling pin, ladle, wooden spoon, slotted spatula, silicone spatulas, potato masher, citrus press, garlic press, cookie cutters, can opener, microplane zester (for peeling citrus skin and grating), salad spinner (to wash greens and fresh herbs), cookie cutters, candy thermometer (to make dough),

Cookware

When in doubt, purchase items that are made from natural sources, such as stainless steel, iron, or enamel. Try to limit your use of non-stick pans; there is some evidence that they may be toxic at high temperatures.

If you can't live without them, limit yourself to one small omelet pan and a large skillet and use them sparingly. Make sure that you use them on low heat and use non-metal tools so that you don't scratch the interior. Once they are chipped, throw them away.

Instead of non-stick bakeware, I recommend using parchment paper, cupcake liners, or the old-fashioned method of greasing your pan.

Parchment Paper to the Rescue

Although it's better for the environment to use as few paper products as possible when cooking, I can't live without parchment paper. It helps food cook evenly, reduces the need for butter or oil, and makes cleaning up a lot easier.

Safety

Keep electrical appliances unplugged at all times except when you are using them. Children under the age of ten should be closely supervised when using appliances.

pastry brush (nylon or silicone last longer), oil mister, skewers, and aprons.

Electrical Appliances that are Worth Every Penny

The following equipment can last for decades if properly cared for.

Food processor. If you can afford only one expensive item, I highly recommend purchasing a food processor. It is very versatile and shortens prep times significantly. If you have a large family, get the twelve-cup model or, if you have limited storage space, try one of the smaller models.

Electric Stand Mixer. If your family loves to bake, an electric stand mixer is a must-have. It is great for making dough, cookie and cake batter, preparing frostings, beating egg whites, and whipping cream.

Immersion blender. This is one of my favorite tools, especially when cooking with or for children. You can prepare smoothies and purée soups in just minutes. While I don't subscribe to "tricking" children, this tool works well for puréeing fruits and vegetables into a smooth consistency that kids are more likely to eat. I recommend one that's mid-priced or higher; otherwise, the motor won't be strong enough to blend quickly or cut through thick ingredients.

How To Freeze Food

For busy parents, frozen, homemade meals can be a major lifesaver. If you'd like to freeze *Easy Meals to Cook with Kids* dishes, here are some suggestions on how to do it properly:

Label Them Well: Use a permanent marker to date the food and describe what it is.

Limit Exposure To Air: Squeeze the air out of bags and wrap items well to prevent freezer burn.

Use Heavy-Duty Bags Or Containers meant for the freezer. Lay them flat in the freezer – remember to keep the oldest foods on top.

Use Them In A Timely Fashion: Some dishes can be frozen for up to nine months to a year if they are wrapped properly. However, it's best to thaw and use dishes within three to six months of freezing.

Defrost Foods Safely: Thaw them in the refrigerator or heat them in a microwave. Do not defrost perishable foods (meat, poultry, fish/seafood, dairy) at room temperature.

Foods That Freeze Well: Soups, stocks, casseroles, bread, nuts, seeds, butter, pasta dishes such as macaroni and cheese and lasagna, pizza and calzones, tomato sauce, pesto, veggie burgers, falafel patties, muffins, pies, cookies, brownies, frosting, raw dough, puff pastry, most meats cooked in sauces, poultry, and raw fish.

Foods That Don't Freeze Well: Sour cream, mayonnaise, fried foods (will become soggy), soft cheeses, yogurt, cooked potatoes, cooked egg whites or egg dishes (which become rubbery).

5

Get Ready to Cook!

The best part of being a cooking teacher is watching my students, both big and small, go from trepidation to confidence in the kitchen. Indeed, some people have an innate flair for cooking but they still need to learn specific skills in order for that talent to manifest. So, go easy on yourself. Even if your first few dishes don't turn out as well as you'd like – keep trying. Most experienced (and honest) chefs will admit that he or she has made plenty of mistakes along the way! Every blunder is an opportunity to learn.

A small group of thoughtful people could change the world. Indeed, it's the only thing that ever has.

Margaret Mead

Try taking a cooking class, with or without your children. Regardless of your culinary experience, classes offer an opportunity to improve your cooking techniques and pick up new recipes. The more comfortable you and your children are in the kitchen, the more likely you'll prepare healthy meals from scratch. Here are some additional suggestions:

Be sure to "mise en place." It's a French phrase that means "everything in its place." In the culinary sense, it means prepping your ingredients and setting everything up before you start cooking in order to have a successful cooking experience. Invest in some small bowls which will allow you and the kids to prep and pre-measure ingredients.

Get in the habit of tasting the dish during the cooking process. Encouraging kids to share their opinion on how to tweak a dish will help them develop a discerning palate.

Place a damp paper towel underneath the cutting board to keep it in place on the countertop while you chop.

Improve your baking skills by learning a few tips. Baked goods typically call for large eggs, not extra large, but you can use either for the recipes in this book. Remember to use dry measuring cups for ingredients like flour and sugar and liquid measuring glasses for oil and water. If you have a convection oven but are unsure how to use it, just remember to decrease the baking time by about five to eight minutes or lower the temperature by about twenty-five degrees.

Don't be discouraged by recipes with lengthy instructions. The recipes in this book include a lot of specific instructions so that novice cooks and children can follow them.

You don't need fancy gadgets to cook great meals. Most of the recipes in this book can be prepared without electrical appliances and expensive tools.

Plan your cooking time accordingly. The preparation time for each recipe in this book reflects how long it would take one adult to make the dish. When preparing these recipes with children, it may take longer or shorter, depending on how old they are.

Be efficient. Maximize your time in the kitchen by cooking multiple meals on the same day.

Adjust recipes according to taste and dietary restrictions. Gluten- and dairy-free recipes are designated with icons:

Gluten-free   (G Free)   Dairy-free   (D Free)

There are a few recipes without icons that can be made dairy- and gluten-free by omitting the cheese and/or by using gluten-free products. (Please note that soy sauce contains gluten!)

Notes

Only where children gather is there any real chance of fun.

Mignon McLaughlin

Chapter 6

De-Lightful Latin Dishes

Go south of the border for a fiesta of flavors and finger foods that kids will love!

Discover ways to incorporate high-fiber items, such as beans and vegetables, into delectable Latin dishes.

Zesty Black Bean and Corn Salad

Prep time: 20 minutes
Total time: 20 minutes
Serves: 4

G Free   D Free

Ingredients

One 15-ounce can black beans (or 2 cups cooked)

2 cups corn kernels (fresh; frozen and thawed; or canned)

2-3 tablespoons red onion, finely diced

¼ teaspoon garlic, minced

3 tablespoons olive oil

2 tablespoons freshly squeezed lemon juice (about 1 lemon)

¼ teaspoon kosher salt or sea salt

Freshly ground pepper to taste

2 tablespoons cilantro, minced

Optional: **minced jalapeño pepper or pinch of chili powder**

I've been teaching this dish to parents and kids for years and it's a hit every time! The best part is that it takes only minutes to prepare. After marinating in the fridge, it tastes even better, making it perfect for after-school snacks. Serve it over grains or salad greens, in tortilla wraps, or as a dip with salsa and corn chips.

Directions

KIDS 8 and up: Clean off the top of the canned beans (and canned corn, if using). Open the can and drain the liquid. Rinse the beans off in a colander and drain well. Combine the beans and the corn in a medium-sized mixing bowl.

KIDS 2 and up: Add the onion and garlic to the beans and corn. In a small bowl, whisk the oil and the lemon juice together and pour over the bean mixture. Stir to combine. Season with salt and pepper. Fold in the cilantro (or serve it separately for picky eaters) and stir. Let the salad stand for 15 minutes (or up to 1 day in the fridge) to allow flavors to blend. This salad is best served at room temperature. Store the salad in a sealed container in the refrigerator for up to 3 days.

Kids Tips

- Serve black beans (or any other beans) and fresh corn kernels as an after-school snack – they make great finger foods!

- The more frequently kids eat beans, the easier time they'll have digesting them (the same goes for adults).

Cooking Tips

- **Removing kernels from fresh corn:** I only buy fresh corn when it's in season **(see page 12)**. To safely remove corn kernels from the cob, slice the wide end of the cob off with a chef's knife (this task is for adults). Then place the now flat-ended cob in a vertical position on a cutting board. Slice off the kernels in a downward motion. Keep cutting around the cob until all the kernels have been removed.

- **Cooking beans from scratch:** Cover beans with plenty of water in a large bowl. Soak them for 8-12 hours in the fridge or at room temperature. Drain the soaking water, put beans in a large stockpot and cover with water (2 cups of water per 1 cup of dried beans). Bring the pot to a boil, lower heat, and simmer beans for about 1 hour or until tender enough that you can mash a cooled bean on the roof of your mouth with your tongue.

- If the corn is frozen, heat it in a small skillet with a little olive oil on low heat for 3-5 minutes.

Creamy Guacamole

Prep time: 15 minutes
Total time: 30 minutes
Serves: 4

Ingredients

2 ripe avocados

1 tablespoon freshly squeezed lime juice
(about 1 lime)

½-1 teaspoon garlic, minced (about 1 garlic clove)

Kosher salt or sea salt to taste

Freshly ground pepper to taste

1 on-the-vine or plum tomato, seeded and diced

2 tablespoons red onion, finely diced

Optional: **½-1 teaspoon jalapeño pepper, finely minced**

Even my pickiest students get excited to prepare guacamole in class! The smooth, buttery texture of avocados is very popular with small eaters. All of the scooping, squeezing, and mashing makes it as much fun to prepare as it is to eat!

Directions

KIDS 6 and up: Cut the avocados in half with a butter knife and remove the pit. While holding half the avocado, scoop out the avocado "flesh" using a spoon. Put the avocado flesh in a medium-sized bowl, discard the skin, and repeat with the other avocado half.

KIDS 2 and up: Mash the avocado with a fork and mix in the lime juice, stirring well until it has reached a creamy consistency. Add the garlic, salt, and pepper. Gently fold in the tomatoes and the red onion (and jalapeño, if using). Chill the guacamole for 15 minutes in the refrigerator to allow flavors to blend. Serve over **Super Spinach and Cheese Quesadillas (page 34)**, with **Crispy Pita Chips (page 86)**, or tortilla chips.

Kids Tips

- If your kids prefer plain avocados, you can halve the avocado, remove the pit, sprinkle it with a little salt, and let them eat it directly out of the skin with a spoon.

- For picky eaters, make a batch of guacamole without red onions and/ or garlic.

Cooking Tips

- The key to luscious guacamole is finding the right avocados. Living in the north, I don't bother buying them between November and March, but if you are in the south, you are very lucky! Look for avocados that are dark green and indent just a little when squeezed. If they are unripe (hard and bright green), store them in a paper bag for a couple of days to speed up the ripening process or put them in the fridge to slow it down.

- When mincing the garlic, add some salt on the cutting board – it makes it easier to mince and also blends the flavors together.

- If you are making this dish a few hours before serving it, store it in the refrigerator with plastic wrap tucked tightly over the guacamole so that it doesn't turn brown.

Elotes
(Mexican Corn-on-the-Cob)

Prep time: 25 minutes
Total time: 25 minutes
Serves: 4

G
Free

Ingredients

4 ears of corn

4 bamboo skewers

4 tablespoons mayonnaise

½ cup Mexican queso fresco or Cotija,
    grated or crumbled

4 teaspoons of freshly squeezed lime juice
    (about 1 lime)

Kosher salt or sea salt to taste

Optional: **chili powder**

The first time I was introduced to this dish by my Mexican friend and instructor, Jacquie Grinberg, I was skeptical about combining mayonnaise, lime juice, cheese and spices on one of my favorite foods. But after my first bite, I was in love and so were my little students – they couldn't get enough of it!

Directions

ADULTS: Break each cob in half. Put a steamer basket in a large, wide pot (that has a tightly-fitting lid) and fill it with a few inches of water. Arrange the corn in the steamer basket so that it's not overcrowded. Cover and steam the corn over medium-high heat for about 15 minutes or until the corn is bright yellow and tender. (If you have access to a grill, you can grill the corn instead.) Let the corn cool down for a few minutes before handling it.

If the cobs are still warm, grab them with a clean dish towel. Drive a bamboo skewer into the wide end of each cob, so that you can hold it without touching the kernels. (Or, you can use corn-on-the-cob holders.)

KIDS 4 and up: With a butter knife, spread approximately 1 tablespoon of mayonnaise onto each cob, coating the kernels generously and evenly.

KIDS 2 and up: Spread cheese on a flat plate or cutting board and roll each cob in about 1-2 tablespoons of cheese, gently pressing the cheese into the mayonnaise. Squeeze about 1 teaspoon of lime juice over each cob. Sprinkle salt (and chili powder, if using) over each cob. Serve immediately. This dish does not store well.

Kids Tips

- Arrange a "dipping" bar with each ingredient so that each family member can customize his or her own cob.

- For kids who don't like mayonnaise, use butter instead, but keep in mind that the cheese won't adhere to the butter as well as it does to mayonnaise.

Cooking Tips

- If you can't find Mexican cheese, substitute grated Monterey jack or Parmesan cheese.

- Steaming and grilling are two healthy cooking techniques but you can also boil the corn too.

Tropical Mango Salsa

Prep time: 15 minutes
Total time: 15 minutes
Yields: 2-3 cups

G Free D Free

Ingredients

2 large mangoes, peeled and cut into cubes

1 cup cherry tomatoes, halved (or 2 roma tomatoes, diced)

¼ cup red onion, finely diced

One 6-ounce can, crushed pineapple

2 tablespoons freshly squeezed lime juice (about 2 limes)

1-2 teaspoons garlic, minced (about 1-2 garlic cloves)

Optional: **½ jalapeño pepper, minced or a pinch of chili powder**

¼ cup packed fresh cilantro, chopped

Kosher salt or sea salt to taste

Freshly ground black pepper

When we make this refreshing recipe in class, the kids often treat it like a fruit salad and eat it with a spoon. Adding fruits to recipes is an excellent way to ease kids into ethnic cuisines. Salsa is packed with nutrients, high in fiber, and can transform any recipe into a colorful, festive dish.

Directions

KIDS 2 and up: Combine mangoes, tomatoes, red onion, pineapple, lime juice, garlic, jalapeño pepper, and cilantro in a bowl (or pulse to desired consistency in a food processor – just be careful that you don't blend it so long that it turns into a liquid). Season with salt and pepper and stir.

Serve salsa with tortilla chips or over **Make-Your-Own Burrito (page 40)**, **Stuffed Mexican Corn Cakes (page 36)**, **Baja Fish Tacos (page 38)**, **Super Spinach and Cheese Quesadillas (page 34)**, or **Mini Black Bean Burgers (page 32)**.

Kids Tips

- Encourage kids to try new tropical fruits in this dish such as guava or papaya, in place of the mango.

Cooking Tips

- You can use any hot chili pepper in place of the jalapeño to add some kick to the dish. Or, omit it if your family doesn't like spicy food.

- If you prefer a sweeter dish, omit the red onions and garlic.

Mini Black Bean Burgers

Prep time: 30 minutes
Total time: 45 minutes
(plus time to bake potato)
Yields: 25 small burgers

D
Free

Ingredients

1 medium sweet potato or yam, baked

Two 15-ounce cans black beans, drained and rinsed

2 scallions, sliced

2 teaspoons garlic, minced (about 2 cloves)

1 egg

½-¾ cup plain breadcrumbs

Kosher salt or sea salt to taste

Freshly ground pepper to taste

2 tablespoons olive oil, for brushing

Optional: **minced jalapeño pepper or crushed red pepper flakes**

2 dozen mini burger buns

Who doesn't love sliders? This dish is always a crowd-pleaser, making it perfect for entertaining. Best of all, they look so much like real burgers that kids don't realize they are eating a nutritious meal that's high in fiber and protein!

Directions

ADULTS: Heat the oven to 375°F. (For instructions on how to bake **potatoes/yams, see page 99.**)

KIDS 4 and up: Peel the cooled sweet potato (or yam), discard the peel, and set aside. Mash the beans and sweet potato in a bowl with a potato masher or fork until roughly half the mixture appears puréed and the other half is still whole beans. Fold in the scallions, garlic, and egg, and stir. Stir in the breadcrumbs. Depending on the size of the potato, you may need to add more breadcrumbs if the mixture is too moist. It should be moist enough to bind together but not so wet that it sticks to your hands. Season with salt and pepper (and jalapeño and red pepper flakes, if using).

KIDS 6 and up: Shape the mixture into approximately 25 small balls of equal size. Flatten each one into a 2½-inch patty and put on a greased baking sheet (or one lined with parchment paper). The patties can be frozen at this point.

KIDS 2 and up: Brush each patty generously with olive oil using a pastry brush.

ADULTS: Bake the patties for about 10 to 12 minutes. Pull the pan out of the oven and, with a thin metal spatula, carefully flip each patty. You can brush them again with oil or just keep cooking them until they are a little crispy around the edges, for 2 to 3 additional minutes. Serve the burgers on buns with **Creamy Guacamole (page 26)** or ketchup. Store the burgers in a sealed container in the refrigerator for up to 4 days or freeze them for up to 6 months.

Kids Tips

- Kids as young as 2 years old can master how to break an egg. **See page 8** for instructions on how to teach **Breaking an Egg.**

Cooking Tips

- You can bake the potato up to 3 days before you prepare the dish – just store it in the fridge until needed.

- Many of my students ask which part of the scallion to use: After cutting off the "hairy" tip, slice the white end until the middle of the green section where the scallion starts to become "floppy" and discard the top green part.

- If you can't find mini burger buns, small dinner rolls or hot dog buns cut in half will work.

Photo by Trevor Frydenlund

Super Spinach and Cheese Quesadillas

Prep time: 15-25 minutes
Total time: 25 minutes
Serves: 3-4

Ingredients

1 tablespoon olive oil or butter

Six 9-inch flour tortillas

1½ cup Cheddar cheese, grated

¼ cup frozen chopped spinach, thawed and drained

Optional: **olive oil for oven method**

I've never met a child who doesn't love quesadillas. You can keep them simple with plain cheese or add gourmet ingredients for more adventurous eaters. If you're too busy to stand at the stove and make one quesadilla at a time, baking them in the oven is a real time-saver.

Directions

STOVETOP METHOD

KIDS 4 and up: Lay three tortillas on a clean surface. Spread the cheese and spinach over each tortilla, leaving a 1-inch border around the edge. Cover each tortilla with a second one to create three quesadilla "sandwiches," and stack them carefully on a large plate next to the stove.

ADULTS: Heat oil or butter in a large skillet over medium-low heat. Carefully put one quesadilla at a time into the pan and cook for about 5-8 minutes until golden and crispy. Flip it and cook for 2-3 more minutes. Repeat this with the other two quesadillas, adding oil or butter to the pan as needed. Cut each one into 8 wedges and serve immediately with **Creamy Guacamole (page 26)**, **Tropical Mango Salsa (page 30)**, and/or sour cream.

OVEN METHOD

ADULTS: Preheat the oven to 350°F degrees.

KIDS 4 and up: Follow the same instructions above to prepare the quesadillas, but instead of stacking them, lay them side-by-side on a greased baking sheet (or one lined with parchment paper). Brush the quesadillas with olive oil using a pastry brush.

ADULTS: Bake the quesadillas for 10-12 minutes until the cheese is melted and the edges are slightly browned.

Kids Tips

- Allow each child to pick out a new vegetable at the grocery store or farmer's market and add it to the quesadillas.

Cooking Tips

- **Thawing and draining spinach:** Thaw spinach by microwaving it in a glass bowl until defrosted. Once it has cooled down, the children can drain the excess water by squeezing small balls of spinach over the sink. Or, you can buy fresh spinach, clean it thoroughly, and wilt it in a sauté pan.

- Other filling options: black beans, diced red peppers, sautéed mushrooms, pesto, feta cheese, goat cheese, kalamata olives, meat or chicken. You get the picture – anything goes! Just make sure you don't overstuff them nor add too little cheese – otherwise, they won't stick together.

- Traditional Mexican quesadillas are made in a dry skillet but I like to use a little butter when making them for kids because it adds some flavor. Feel free to omit it and cook them in a dry pan.

Stuffed Mexican Corn Cakes

Prep time: 35 minutes
Total time: 35 minutes
Yields: 10-12 corn cakes

G
Free

Ingredients

1½ cups masa harina (corn flour)

1 cup water

1 teaspoon kosher salt or sea salt

2-3 teaspoons olive oil

⅓ cup Cheddar cheese, grated

⅓ cup kidney beans or black beans

2 tablespoons canola oil, for pan

Optional: **diced peppers, corn, sautéed greens**

This creative yet simple recipe is so well-liked by kids that I chose to prepare it on *Sesame Street* with my students. You can use any ingredient for the filling as long as it can be diced into tiny pieces. Serve the corn cakes at dinner parties as a gourmet appetizer for adults and a main entrée for children.

Directions

KIDS 2 and up: In a medium-sized bowl, combine the masa harina, water, salt, and olive oil, and stir with a wooden spoon. Work the dough together until it's a firm ball. If it's dry, add a few drops of water.

KIDS 6 and up: Create small balls of dough about 2½-inches in diameter and put them on a greased baking sheet (or one lined with parchment paper), leaving space between them. Flatten them into patties about 3 inches in diameter and about ¼-inch thick.

KIDS 2 and up: Press your thumb directly into the center of each patty to form a wide, shallow indentation about half as deep as the patty. If the patties crack at this point, add a few drops of water to the cracks and pinch the dough together to smooth out the surface. In each indentation, add a total of 1 teaspoon of cheese and beans (or optional ingredients, if using). Then, fold the dough over the indentation and re-shape each patty so that the filling is all covered up. Make sure that the patties are only ¼-inch thick so that they will cook through the middle.

ADULTS: Heat a skillet (iron skillets work best) over medium-high heat and add enough oil to coat the bottom of the pan. Add some corn cakes to the pan without overcrowding it. After 3-4 minutes, flip each corn cake and cook the other side. Finish cooking all of the corn cakes, adding more oil if needed. Each side should be a little golden brown but still mostly light yellow. Serve the cakes hot with **Creamy Guacamole (page 26), Tropical Mango Salsa (page 30)**, and/or sour cream. Store the cakes in a sealed container in the refrigerator for up to 4 days.

Kids Tips

- Make sure that kids don't add too much filling or it will ooze out during the cooking process.

Cooking Tips

- Masa harina can be found at many major grocery stores. Maseca and Bob's Red Mill are two popular brands.

Recipe by Julie Negrin and Jacquie Grinberg

Baja Fish Tacos with White Sauce

Prep time: 30 minutes
Total time: 45 minutes
Yields: 10-12 tacos

Ingredients

2 tablespoons freshly squeezed lime juice
(about 2 limes)

2 tablespoons olive oil

1 tablespoon wheat-free tamari or soy sauce

1 pound white fish (tilapia, cod, or halibut)

½ cup shredded cabbage

4 leaves romaine, sliced

1 medium-sized carrot, grated

¼ cup red onion, diced

Kosher salt or sea salt to taste

Freshly ground pepper to taste

8-12 corn tortillas or taco shells

Optional: **grated cheese or salsa**

White Sauce

¼ cup mayonnaise (or plain yogurt)

1 tablespoon freshly squeezed lime juice
(about 1 lime)

2 tablespoons chopped cilantro

1 clove garlic, pressed
(or 1 teaspoon minced garlic)

1 tablespoon water

Optional: **⅛ teaspoon cumin**

Even my students who say they don't like fish confess that they love this recipe. The list of ingredients is long but the recipe is actually simple to prepare. To mix it up, try replacing the fish with black beans or grilled chicken. Keep the ingredients in the fridge all week for instant "taco night" dinners.

Directions

ADULTS: Preheat the broiler. Slice the fish into pieces that are 4 inches long and 1½-inches wide (or have a fishmonger do it for you) and put them into a baking dish.

KIDS 6 and up: Whisk 1 tablespoon each of the lime juice, olive oil and tamari together in a small bowl and pour the mixture over the fish. Allow the fish to marinate for 15-30 minutes in the refrigerator. Meanwhile, prepare the vegetables and put them in a medium-sized bowl. In a separate small bowl, combine the remaining 1 tablespoon of olive oil and lime juice, salt, and pepper and pour it over the vegetables.

ADULTS: Transfer the marinated fish to a baking sheet (or a broiler pan) lined with foil and place it approximately 5 inches underneath the broiler (the heat source at the top of the oven). Broil the fish for 8-10 minutes until the center of the largest piece is cooked through and flakes easily. Warm the tortillas in a skillet or in the oven.

KIDS 4 and up: In a small bowl, combine the mayonnaise (or yogurt), lime juice, cilantro, garlic, water, (and cumin, if using), and stir them together until smooth. Put 1-2 fish pieces in each tortilla and top with dressed vegetables and white sauce. (Add a little grated cheese and salsa, if using.) Repeat this process for each tortilla. Serve immediately. Store the fish, vegetables, and white sauce in separate, sealed containers in the refrigerator for up to 4 days.

Kids Tips

- Put kids in charge of setting up the "taco bar" and encourage them to use different vegetables, beans, spices, and other ingredients in their tacos.

Cooking Tips

- The broiler is very hot so don't use parchment paper when broiling, and keep a close eye on the fish so that it doesn't burn.

- It's not necessary to spend a lot of money on the white fish you purchase for this recipe, but if you can, buy wild fish (versus farm-raised) from a reputable fishmonger.

Recipe adapted from *Feeding the Whole Family* by Cynthia Lair (Sasquatch Books; 3rd edition, 2008)

Make-Your-Own Burrito Bar with Brown Rice

Prep time: 25 minutes
Total time: 1 hour
Serves: 6

Ingredients

Six 9-inch flour tortillas

One 15-ounce can of white, black, or kidney beans

2 cups cooked brown rice (see instructions below)

2 cups any combination, cooked and raw vegetables

1 cup jack cheese, grated

Optional: **cooked chicken, beef or fish**

Brown Rice

1½ cups short- or long-grain brown rice

3 cups water

Burritos are the perfect meal for families that can't agree on what to have for dinner. They're also an excellent way to use up leftover vegetables and meat. Try adding whatever is in season, such as sautéed kale and sweet potato in the cold months or fresh corn and tomatoes in the summer.

Directions

KIDS 8 and up: Clean off the top of the canned beans. Open the can and drain the liquid. Rinse the beans in a colander and drain well.

KIDS 6 and up: Place each ingredient in a separate bowl and line them up along a counter or table that children can reach. On a large plate, lay your tortilla flat. Spoon the desired ingredients into the center of the tortilla. Make sure that it's not so full that you can't close it up. Fold the sides and ends of the tortilla towards the center and flip the burrito over onto a plate so that each side is tucked underneath. Top with **Creamy Guacamole (page 26), Tropical Mango Salsa (page 30),** and/or sour cream.

Brown Rice

ADULTS: In a fine-meshed strainer, rinse the rice under cold, running water for a couple of minutes. In a medium saucepan that has a tightly-fitting lid, combine the rice and water.

Raise the heat to high and bring it to a boil, then turn the heat down and cover the pan (you can leave the lid slightly ajar so that the water doesn't bubble over). Do not stir the rice while it's cooking. Cook the rice for about 35-40 minutes or until there is no remaining water. Remove the pan from the heat and let the rice sit for about 10 minutes, then fluff with a fork and serve immediately. Leftovers will keep in the refrigerator for up to 5 days in a sealed container. Add a little water when re-heating the rice.

Kids Tips

- If brown rice is new to children, burritos are the perfect opportunity to introduce it, since the rice is mixed in with other ingredients. If kids are still reluctant to taste brown rice, try mixing it with some white rice to ease them into the flavor and texture.

- Encourage kids to be in charge of deciding on the burrito fillings so that they are more likely to try new ingredients.

Cooking Tips

- Burrito-filling options: diced red pepper, sliced tomatoes, sautéed leafy greens, caramelized onions, roasted eggplant, and steamed broccoli or cauliflower.

- In order to determine when a whole grain is done cooking, slide a butter knife down the side of the pan and carefully pull the grain away from the side to see if there is any water on the bottom of the pan. Once there is just a small amount of water on the bottom of the pan, turn off the heat and allow it to finish steaming, covered on the stove for about 10 minutes before fluffing and serving.

Notes

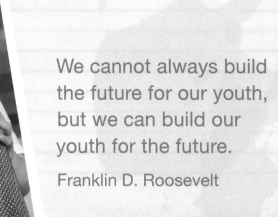

We cannot always build the future for our youth, but we can build our youth for the future.

Franklin D. Roosevelt

Chapter 7

Enticing Italian Fare

Everybody loves Italian food – especially kids!

It's a cheese-heavy cuisine but there are lots of opportunities to balance it out with nutritious ingredients like fresh herbs and vegetables.

Best Ever Caesar Salad

Prep time: 25 minutes
Total time: 25 minutes
Yields: ½ cup dressing

Ingredients

2 small heads romaine lettuce

1 tablespoon red wine vinegar

⅛ teaspoon Worcestershire sauce

1 tablespoon freshly squeezed lemon juice (about ½ lemon)

2 cloves of garlic, finely minced (about 2 cloves)

1 teaspoon anchovy paste or 3-4 fillets, finely minced

3½ tablespoons mayonnaise

⅓ cup olive oil

Freshly ground pepper to taste

½-1 cup grated Parmesan cheese

Crunchy Croutons (page 46)

Who doesn't love Caesar salad? My students get very excited when they find out we are making this recipe in class! It's an ideal way to introduce children to eating salad greens. You can also use the dressing for other salads or as a dip so that kids will eat more vegetables.

Directions

KIDS 2 and up: Wash the lettuce and dry it well in a salad spinner or a clean towel. Tear the lettuce into bite-sized pieces.

KIDS 6 and up: Whisk the red wine vinegar, Worcestershire sauce, lemon juice, garlic, anchovies, and mayonnaise together. Continue to whisk while slowly adding the olive oil. Stir in the black pepper.

KIDS 2 and up: Just before serving, toss the lettuce leaves with half of the dressing. You can add more dressing according to taste and how much lettuce you are using. Garnish the salad with Parmesan cheese and croutons. Store the dressing in a sealed container in the refrigerator for up to a week.

Kids Tips

- Dip a piece of lettuce into the dressing and taste it in order to see if it needs more garlic, lemon juice or anchovies, depending on your family's taste.

- Let the kids offer guests extra ground pepper – many kids adore using a pepper grinder.

- Kids who aren't sensitive to strong smells can chop up the anchovies and garlic. If they don't like the idea of eating anchovies, just slip in some anchovy paste for the adult batch or omit it.

Cooking Tips

- Take the time to squeeze fresh lemon juice and grate high-quality Parmesan instead of using pre-grated cheese and lemon juice concentrate – it will make a big difference in taste.

- If you prefer a thicker dressing, whisk in 2 tablespoons of freshly grated Parmesan.

- Make a double batch of the dressing so that you can serve it with veggie sticks as an after-school snack.

  Thank you, Nancy Woodward, for inspiring this recipe!

Crunchy Croutons

Prep time: 10 minutes
Total time: 25 minutes
Yields: 3-4

Ingredients

4 pieces of stale, white or whole wheat bread

⅓ cup olive oil

1-2 tablespoons grated Parmesan cheese

¼ teaspoon kosher salt or sea salt

Bite-sized croutons add some kid-friendly fun to salads. Although children often prefer their foods separate, many of my students make an exception for the Caesar salad and Panzanella (Tomato and Bread Salad) because they find small pieces of bread mixed in with vegetables irresistible.

Directions

ADULTS: Preheat the oven to 425°F.

KIDS 8 and up: Cut the bread into uniform 1-inch cubes. Spread them evenly on a greased baking sheet (or one lined with parchment paper). Drizzle the olive oil over the bread cubes.

KIDS 2 and up: Toss the bread cubes with your hands to coat each piece with olive oil. Sprinkle on the Parmesan cheese and salt.

ADULTS: Bake the bread cubes for 10-15 minutes or until they are golden-brown and crispy.

Cherry Tomato Caprese Skewers

Prep time: 10 minutes
Total time: 10 minutes
Serves: 6

G
Free

Ingredients

- **1 small bunch fresh basil**
- **15-20 bocconcini** (bite-sized mozzarella balls)
- **1 pint cherry or grape tomatoes**
- **2 tablespoons olive oil**
- **Kosher salt or sea salt to taste**
- **Freshly ground pepper to taste**
- **Bamboo skewers or toothpicks**
- Optional: **balsamic vinegar**

This quick'n'easy recipe was inspired by my friend, Carin Brody, and is always a favorite with both kids and adults. In the warmer months, my little students use the colorful orange, yellow, and red cherry tomatoes that are bursting with flavor.

Directions

KIDS 2 and up: Clean the basil well and dry it in a salad spinner or in a clean dish towel. Carefully, tear the basil leaves off their stems. Set aside.

KIDS 8 and up: Carefully slide one bocconcini, a basil leaf, and a cherry tomato onto a skewer (or colorful toothpick). Repeat this until each skewer is full. Lay the skewers in a wide dish. Drizzle each skewer with a little olive oil (and the balsamic vinegar, if using). Season with salt and pepper and serve immediately.

Perfect Panzanella
(Tomato and Bread Salad)

Prep time: 25 minutes
Total time: 25 minutes
Serves: 4

D
Free

Ingredients

3 on-the-vine or plum tomatoes, diced

1 red pepper, diced

½ English cucumber, peeled and diced

2-3 tablespoons red onion, finely diced

½ ciabatta or any rustic bread, cubed (about 2 cups)

4-5 basil leaves, shredded

Optional: **basil and/or fresh mozzarella, grated**

Dressing

2 tablespoons red wine vinegar

2 teaspoons balsamic vinegar

1 teaspoon Dijon mustard

½ teaspoon garlic, minced (about 1 clove)

¼ cup olive oil

¼ teaspoon kosher salt or sea salt

Freshly ground pepper to taste

To help my students remain open-minded about salads, I find inventive ways to describe a dish. They like the idea of making something exotic-sounding like "panzanella" and happily eat their vegetables and cubed bread without complaint. Since this is such a popular recipe, I added in red pepper and cucumbers for extra nutrients and fiber.

Directions

KIDS 6 and up: In a large bowl, combine the tomatoes, red pepper, cucumber, and red onion. In a separate bowl, whisk the red wine vinegar, balsamic vinegar, Dijon mustard, garlic, olive oil, salt and pepper together until well-combined.

KIDS 2 and up: Add the bread cubes to the vegetables and pour the dressing over the ingredients. Toss the salad until everything is well-coated. Gently fold in the basil (and the mozzarella cheese, if using). Serve immediately or allow the salad to sit for about 20 minutes to allow the flavors to blend. Store it in a sealed container in the refrigerator (without the bread, which will become soggy) for up to 2 days.

Kids Tips

- Many kids enjoy the task of tearing up the bread – just make sure their pieces are roughly the same size.

- If your kids prefer milder flavors, omit the red onion and basil.

- For added protein and to make it a complete meal, toss in some white beans or chicken.

Cooking Tips

- You can use the **Crunchy Croutons (page 46)** in place of the cubed bread.

- It's best to use stale bread for this dish. If you buy a fresh loaf for this recipe, leave it uncovered on the counter for a couple of days before preparing the salad.

- English cucumbers are much longer than regular cucumbers so this recipe would need one regular cucumber in place of one half of an English cucumber.

- This recipe doesn't yield a huge amount since it will become soggy a couple hours after the bread is added. If you want to make this dish for a party, double the ingredients and add the bread half an hour before serving it.

Cheesy Garlic Bread

Prep time: 5 minutes
Total time: 15 minutes
Yields: 12 pieces

Ingredients

½ baguette

2 garlic cloves, halved

2 tablespoons olive oil

1 cup mozzarella cheese, shredded

This recipe is perfect for breakfast or after-school snacks when you're short on patience and ingredients. For a more sophisticated dish, transform this recipe into bruschetta by topping toasted bread with diced tomatoes, fresh basil, artichoke hearts, white beans, or roasted eggplant. Drizzle it with a little olive oil and balsamic vinegar and serve.

Directions

ADULTS: Heat the oven to 350°F. With a serrated knife, cut the bread into 1-inch slices.

KIDS 4 and up: Place the bread pieces on a greased baking sheet (or one lined with parchment paper). Rub garlic halves on each slice of bread. Brush each piece of bread with olive oil. Sprinkle the cheese on top.

ADULTS: Bake for 6-8 minutes until the cheese is melted and the bread is golden around the edges.

Kids Tips

- Encourage kids to try different cheese, herb, and vegetable combinations, such as feta, oregano, and tomatoes.

Cooking Tips

- If you don't have fresh garlic, use crushed garlic or garlic powder.

Quick Cookin' Gourmet Mac-n-Cheese

Prep time: 25 minutes
Total time: 35 minutes
Serves: 8-10

Ingredients

1 pound elbow pasta or macaroni

¼ cup butter (½ stick)

3 tablespoons unbleached, all-purpose flour

½ teaspoon dry mustard

¼ teaspoon ground nutmeg

2½ cups whole milk

3 cups sharp Cheddar cheese, grated

½ cup Parmesan cheese, grated

½ teaspoon kosher salt or sea salt

Freshly ground pepper to taste

This dish takes almost the same amount of time to prepare as the boxed version but is made with whole foods and tastes much better. Many of the ingredients are regular pantry items, making it convenient for busy weekday nights. Try freezing single portions in sealed containers for lunch boxes and after-school snacks.

Directions

ADULTS: Cook the noodles according to package directions. When the noodles are almost done cooking, melt the butter in a separate medium-sized saucepan over low heat. Add the flour to the butter and stir for about 2-3 minutes. Mix in the dry mustard and nutmeg, combine well, and cook for 2 more minutes.

Add the milk to the butter mixture and bring it to a boil, stirring frequently to make sure that it does not burn. Once the milk starts to bubble up and come to a boil, stir continuously for 2 minutes until it thickens. Remove the pan from the heat. When the noodles are done cooking, drain them in a colander in the sink and transfer them to a large mixing bowl.

KIDS 8 and up: Carefully add both cheeses to the milk mixture in the pan. Stir until the cheese is fully melted and the mixture is smooth and creamy. Pour it over the noodles, season with salt and pepper, and stir to combine. The mac-n-cheese can be stored in a sealed container in the refrigerator for up to 5 days or in the freezer for up to 6 months.

Kids Tips

- Since this dish is mostly prepared on the stove, the kids can measure the flour, salt, mustard, nutmeg, and milk in advance so that they're ready to be added to the pan.

- Pre-grated cheese is useful in a pinch but it can sometimes separate in the sauce and make it grainy. Instead, enlist the older kids to grate cheese for this dish.

- This recipe yields plenty of leftovers since this dish is so popular with children.

Cooking Tips

- Whole milk works best in this recipe, though you can substitute lower fat milk products.

- This recipe relies on both Cheddar and Parmesan cheese, which most families already have in their fridge. For a more gourmet touch, replace the Parmesan with Gruyère or Swiss cheese.

On-the-Go Frittata Squares

Prep time: 30 minutes
Total time: 1 hour
Serves: 4-6

G
Free

Ingredients

1 tablespoon olive oil

1 small yellow onion, finely diced

1 cup grape or cherry tomatoes, halved

1 cup fresh baby spinach leaves, chopped

10 eggs

1 cup grated Parmesan cheese

1 teaspoon kosher salt or sea salt

½ teaspoon freshly ground black pepper

1-2 tablespoons fresh basil, shredded

Cooking spray or olive oil mister to grease pan

Optional: **extra basil for garnish**

A frittata is a baked egg dish that works well for hectic weeknight meals when you have only a few ingredients on hand. Make it seasonal by adding sautéed squash, eggplant, leeks, or different cheeses and fresh herbs. This dish is ideal when you're on the run, because you can cut it into squares, store them in a baggie, and eat them without utensils!

Directions

ADULTS: Preheat the oven to 350°F. Heat the oil in a skillet over medium heat and cook the onions until translucent, about 10-12 minutes. Add the tomatoes and cook them until softened, about 5-6 minutes. Remove the pan from the heat and stir in the spinach, which will wilt in the still-warm pan. Allow the vegetables to cool for 5-10 minutes.

KIDS 4 and up: In a large mixing bowl, beat the eggs, cheese, salt, and pepper together. Stir the spinach, tomatoes, and basil into the eggs.

ADULTS: Spray an 8-inch pan with cooking spray or olive oil mister. Pour the egg batter into the greased pan. Bake until the center of the frittata is set and the edges start to brown, 30-35 minutes. Remove the frittata from the oven and allow it to cool for 5-10 minutes. Cut it into squares and serve immediately. Store the squares in a sealed container in the refrigerator for 2-3 days.

Kids Tips

- If tomatoes aren't in season, have the kids pick out a seasonal vegetable from the store or farmer's market.

- Let the kids garnish or "decorate" the top of the frittata with the tomatoes and basil before it goes into the oven (smiley faces are always popular).

- Kids as young as 2 years old can master how to break an egg. **See page 8** for instructions on how to teach **Breaking an Egg.**

Cooking Tips

- If you have picky eaters, make a "kids' half" of the frittata just as you would with a pizza. Cook fewer vegetables, pour the egg mixture into the pan without the vegetables and add vegetables to only one-half of the pan.

- If you don't have fresh spinach, you can substitute approximately ½ cup of frozen spinach that has been thawed and drained.

- For meat eaters, you could add in crumbled turkey bacon for extra flavor and protein.

- This is the perfect recipe for using up leftover vegetables in your fridge.

Recipe by Julie Negrin and Adeena Sussman

Caramelized Onion and Roasted Red Pepper Pizza

Prep time: 25 minutes (plus onion, dough and sauce prep time)
Total time: 1¼ hours
Serves: 4-6

Ingredients

1 tablespoon vegetable oil

1 batch Pizza Dough (page 58)

¾ cup Basic Basil Tomato Sauce (page 60)

3 cups shredded mozzarella cheese

2 cups grated Cheddar cheese

Toppings

1 red onion, sliced and caramelized
     (see next page)

1 Roasted Red Pepper (page 91)**, sliced**

One 8-ounce can black olives, sliced

Making pizza from scratch is a lot more fun than ordering take-out. When using homemade tomato sauce and vitamin-packed vegetable toppings, pizza can be quite nutritious. Prepare your own mouthwatering toppings for the gourmands and keep the other half of the pizza cheese-only for the picky eaters.

Directions

ADULTS: Preheat the oven to 450°F.

KIDS 4 and up: Rub oil on a 12½ -inch by 17½-inch baking sheet. Place the dough in the middle of the pan and use your fingers to push it outward toward the edges until it covers the entire pan. Make sure that it is distributed evenly. Pinch the edges to create a small crust all the way around. (At this point, you can bake the dough by itself for 5 minutes, if you prefer a crisper crust.)

KIDS 4 and up: Spread the sauce over the dough to the edge of the crust and sprinkle with cheese and toppings.

ADULTS: Bake the pizza for 8-10 minutes or until the crust turns golden. Allow pizza to cool for 10-15 minutes and then cut it into squares and serve. You can store the pizza in a sealed container in the refrigerator for up to 4 days or you can also freeze leftovers for up to 6 months in a sealed container or ziptop bag.

Kids Tips

- Encourage kids to be in charge of "decorating" the pizza and to try new vegetables on their side of the pizza as their palates mature. Experiment with unusual toppings such as steamed broccoli or slices of baked sweet potatoes, russet potatoes, or pumpkin. For birthday parties, make dessert pizzas with sliced fruit and cinnamon sugar.

- Other topping ideas: chopped herbs, feta cheese, goat cheese, fresh mozzarella, kalamata olives, salami, pepperoni, artichoke hearts, olive tapenade, pesto, fontina, or sautéed greens.

Cooking Tips

- **How to caramelize onions:** Heat 1 tablespoon of olive oil in a stainless steel or cast iron skillet (non-stick pans are not the best option for caramelizing). Cook onions over medium heat, stirring to prevent sticking, until they are translucent, for about 15 minutes. Reduce the heat to medium-low and cook the onions, stirring frequently, until they reduce in size and have turned deep brown, about 45 minutes to 1 hour. If the onions stick to the pan or if they brown unevenly, add 1-2 tablespoons of water.

- In a pinch, you can buy pre-made pizza dough.

- If your family enjoys making homemade pizza, it is worthwhile to purchase a pizza stone and pizza peel.

Photo by Trevor Frydenlund

Pizza and Calzone Dough

Prep time: 20-25 minutes
Total time: 1½ hours
Yields: 1 large pizza or 6 medium-sized calzones

D
Free

Ingredients

1 teaspoon active dry yeast

½ teaspoon sugar

1 cup warm water

1 teaspoon kosher salt or sea salt

2½ cups unbleached, all-purpose flour

1 tablespoon olive oil

1 teaspoon vegetable oil for the bowl

Extra flour for kneading

Once you get the hang of preparing homemade dough, it's a cinch to make and the taste is unbeatable. While some kids aren't very interested in cooking, making dough seems to be a universally-loved activity. Best of all, the ingredients don't cost much.

Directions

KIDS 2 and up: In a large glass, combine the yeast and sugar. Add the warm water (approximately 105°-110°F). Let the mixture stand for about 10 minutes until it "proofs" (becomes frothy and creamy). In a large mixing bowl, combine <u>only 1 cup</u> of flour with the salt. Pour the proofed yeast into the flour mixture and add the olive oil. Stir the ingredients together with a wooden spoon.

KIDS 6 and up: Very gradually add more flour – only ¼ cup at a time – until the mixture starts to bind together and resemble dough. You may not need the full 2½ cups (or you may need a little more): the dough is ready when it's still sticky but dry enough that you can handle it with your hands.

KIDS 2 and up: Work the dough into a round ball. It will still be very sticky, which is okay. Sprinkle a couple of pinches of flour on a dry, clean surface and use this area to knead the dough for about 5-8 minutes until it comes together in a smooth, round ball. (**See page 8** for instructions on **How to Knead Dough.**)

KIDS 6 and up: Wipe out the bowl, rub it with a little oil, and place the dough inside. Cover the bowl with a dish towel or plastic wrap so that a "skin" doesn't form on top of the dough.

Let the dough rise for 45 minutes to 1 hour in a warm room until it doubles in bulk.

KIDS 2 and up: Once the dough has risen, "punch" it down to remove any air bubbles, and knead it for 3-5 minutes. Once you no longer feel any air bubbles in the dough, form it into a ball, and it's ready to be made into **Pizza (page 56)** or **Calzones (62).**

Kids Tips

- Make sure the kids don't add too much flour or the dough will end up too dry.

- "Punching down dough" is exactly what it sounds like – make fists with your hands and punch down the dough for 2-3 minutes.

Cooking Tips

- If you're unfamiliar with proofing yeast, buy an inexpensive candy thermometer to test the temperature of the water. Too much heat will kill the yeast and too little will prevent it from activating.

- Make sure that you buy Active Yeast (not rapid rise or instant yeast), store it in the fridge, and keep an eye on the expiration date.

- If you want to make the dough in advance: Store it in the fridge in a sealed bag (instead of letting it rise in a bowl) for at least 12 hours or up to 3 days. Remove it from the fridge, punch it down, and let it rise again in a bowl at room temperature for about 1 hour. Form it into pizza or calzones and bake.

- For a heartier crust, you can replace up to half of the flour in this recipe with whole wheat flour.

- For dedicated dough-makers, it's worth investing in a Danish dough hook, which is like a fancy whisk designed specifically to prepare dough.

Basic Basil Tomato Sauce

Prep time: 30 minutes
Total time: 1½ - 2½ hours
Yields: 7-8 cups

Ingredients

2 tablespoons olive oil

3 yellow onions, diced

3 cloves garlic, minced (about 3 cloves)

2-3 stalks celery, diced

1 large carrot or 10 baby carrots, diced

One 14-ounce can of tomato sauce

**One 28-ounce can of diced or
    crushed tomatoes**

1 bay leaf

1 tablespoon fresh oregano (or 1 teaspoon dried)

1 tablespoon fresh thyme (or 1 teaspoon dried)

4 tablespoons fresh basil (or 2 teaspoons dried)

1-2 teaspoons dried Italian Seasoning

1-2 cups water

Kosher salt or sea salt to taste

Freshly ground pepper to taste

Optional: **bell peppers, zucchini, mushrooms,
    or additional fresh herbs, chopped**

If you're worried that your children aren't eating enough vegetables, puréed sauces are a fantastic opportunity to add some nutrient-packed produce into their diet. Many parents admit that they didn't think they'd ever bother with making homemade sauce – until they tried this recipe!

Directions

ADULTS: In an 8-quart stockpot or Dutch oven, heat the oil on medium heat. Cook the onions on low heat until translucent, about 10-12 minutes. Stir in the garlic, celery, carrots and any other vegetables, and cook for 15 more minutes, stirring frequently. Add the tomato sauce, crushed or diced tomatoes, bay leaf, half the fresh herbs, the spices, and water and bring it to a boil.

Turn the heat down to low, and simmer for at least 30 minutes or up to 2 hours. You may need to add water since the sauce thickens while it cooks. Stir frequently, especially if you don't have a heavy-bottomed pan. Season with salt and pepper. Remove the sauce from the heat and take out the bay leaf. Add the rest of the fresh herbs and stir well.

KIDS 8 and up: To create a smooth texture, purée the sauce with a hand-held immersion blender (or in a regular blender once it's cooled down). This sauce can be used for pizza, calzones, pasta, lasagna, manicotti, or eggplant Parmesan. You can store it for up to 5 days in the refrigerator or up to 6 months in the freezer.

Kids Tips

- If you allow the older kids to help purée the sauce, make sure that it's not hot anymore! If they are using an immersion blender, it's a good idea for them to wear a large oven mitt to protect their arms in case the sauce splatters.

- The kids can pick the fresh herbs off their stems, cut the vegetables, and open the canned tomatoes.

Cooking Tips

- You don't need every single vegetable or herb in order to prepare this recipe – but the onions are a must. Try making **Caramelized Onions (page 57)** to create a richer tasting sauce.

- This recipe yields more than you'll need for one meal so that you can freeze the leftovers in dinner-sized portions. Don't forget to date them!

- Use up your wilting vegetables and bruised tomatoes for this recipe instead of letting them go to waste.

- Italian Seasoning is a mixture of basil, oregano, thyme, marjoram and other herbs.

Three-Cheese Spinach Calzones

Prep time: 45 minutes (plus dough and sauce prep time)
Total time: 50 minutes
Yields: 6 calzones

Ingredients

1 tablespoon olive oil

½ yellow onion, diced

1¼ cup ricotta cheese

½ cup shredded mozzarella cheese

½ cup grated Parmesan cheese

¾-1 cup frozen spinach, thawed and drained (about 6-8 ounces)

½ teaspoon garlic, minced (about 1 small clove)

⅛ teaspoon ground nutmeg

¼ teaspoon kosher salt or sea salt

Fresh ground pepper to taste

Optional: **replace ½ cup cheese with ½ cup of crumbled firm tofu** (raw or cooked)

1 batch Calzone dough (page 58)

2-3 tablespoons olive oil, for brushing

1½ cups Basic Basil Tomato Sauce (page 60) **for dipping**

Calzones, which are like pizza pockets, are a perfect on-the-go meal because they can be quickly reheated or served at room temperature. Like many recipes in this book, you can adjust the ingredients according to season and to your family's taste – try adding mushrooms, eggplant, pumpkin, roasted peppers, or cooked meat to the filling.

Directions

ADULTS: Preheat the oven to 450°F. In a small skillet, heat the olive oil over medium heat and cook the onion until translucent, 10-12 minutes. (Onions can be omitted if you're short on time.) Allow them to cool and set aside.

KIDS 4 and up: While the onions are cooking, combine the ricotta, mozzarella, and Parmesan cheese in a medium-sized bowl. Add the spinach, garlic, nutmeg, salt, and pepper and stir together. Fold in the cooked onions (and tofu or other ingredients, if using).

KIDS 6 and up: Divide the dough into 6 balls. Dust a rolling pin and flat surface with a pinch of flour (too much will dry out the dough). Roll out each ball of dough into a 7-inch circle. Spoon 1/3 cup of filling onto one-half of the dough circle, so that it resembles a half-moon, leaving a border for the edge. Fold the other half of the dough over the filling and press the edges together.

KIDS 4 and up: Thoroughly seal each calzone by using your fingertips to crimp the edges together. Press down the edges with fork tines for decoration. (At this point, calzones can be frozen.) Poke the tops of the calzones 2 or 3 times with a fork to create air holes. Place the calzones on a greased baking sheet (or one lined with parchment paper) and brush each calzone with olive oil.

ADULTS: Bake the calzones until golden brown, for 15-18 minutes. Before serving to small children, allow calzones to cool a little bit since the filling will be very hot. Serve calzones with the **Basic Basil Tomato Sauce (page 60)** for dipping. Store the calzones in a sealed container in the refrigerator for up to 4 days or freeze for up to 6 months.

Kids Tips

- If your kids are wheat-and-dairy fiends, calzones are the perfect opportunity to slip some extra vegetables and protein into their diet.

- Small kids often love using rolling pins, pressing the edges of the calzones with a fork, and using a pastry brush to "paint" the oil on top.

Cooking Tips

- It's easier to buy frozen spinach in a bag rather than a box so that you can take out what you need and put the bag back in the freezer.

Notes

We must teach our
children to dream with
their eyes open.

Harry Edwards

Chapter 8

Appetizing Asian Cuisine

Transport yourself to the exotic Far East . . .

. . . as you create tempting, Asian dishes made with nutrient-packed ingredients such as tofu, edamame, miso, and soba noodles.

Poppin' Edamame Salad

Prep time: 15 minutes
Total time: 25 minutes
Serves: 4

G Free   **D** Free

Ingredients

**One 10-ounce bag of shelled edamame,
frozen**

1 cup corn kernels (fresh; frozen
and thawed; or canned)

1 large carrot or 10 baby carrots, diced

1 tablespoon freshly squeezed lemon juice
(about ½ lemon)

1 tablespoon mirin

2 teaspoons rice vinegar

3 tablespoons toasted sesame oil

⅛ teaspoon kosher salt or sea salt

Freshly ground pepper to taste

Optional: **1 tablespoon fresh cilantro, chopped**

After a few years in the classroom, I discovered that most kids will eat just about anything, including grains and vegetables, once it's been drizzled with toasted sesame oil. This dish is high in protein and takes very little time to prepare. It can be served cold or at room temperature, which makes it convenient for lunch boxes.

Directions

ADULTS: Cook the edamame according to package directions. Drain and transfer the edamame to a medium-sized bowl to cool for about 10 minutes.

KIDS 2 and up: Add corn and carrots to the edamame. In a separate bowl, whisk the lemon juice, mirin, rice vinegar and sesame oil together. Pour the dressing over the vegetables and stir to combine. Season with salt and pepper (and fold in the cilantro, if using). Serve immediately or store in the refrigerator for up to 5 days in a sealed container.

Kids Tips

- Many kids enjoy squeezing lemons. Don't be surprised if they eat the lemon right off the rind. I've found that many kids love it even though it's sour.

- Young kids can tear cilantro leaves off the stems, but only the older children or an adult should be in charge of peeling and cutting the carrots.

Cooking Tips

- You can buy a pre-cooked brand of edamame to shorten the preparation time.

- If the corn is frozen, heat it in a small skillet with a little olive oil on low heat for 3-5 minutes.

- If you are using fresh corn, you'll need about 2 ears. **See page 25** for directions on how to remove kernels from a cob.

- Try adding in different vegetables, depending on the season: sautéed butternut squash in the cool months or sautéed broccoli rabe in the warmer months.

- If you don't have mirin (a sweet rice wine and wonderful alternative sweetener), substitute honey or maple syrup.

Sweet-n-Sour Tofu Bites

Prep time: 20 minutes
Total time: 35 minutes
Serves: 2-4

G Free   D Free

Ingredients

1 pound tofu (firm or extra firm)

1 tablespoon vegetable oil

4 tablespoons wheat-free tamari or soy sauce

4 tablespoons all-natural maple syrup

4 tablespoons water

Adults and kids who claim that they don't like tofu end up chowing down on this dish. Tofu is a very kid-friendly product; with its neutral flavor and smooth texture, it can be adapted to any recipe. Unless you are preparing tofu in a soup or sauce, make sure you drain it well before cooking it.

Directions

KIDS 6 and up: Drain the water from the tofu package. Wrap the tofu in a clean dishtowel or cheesecloth for at least 10 minutes to absorb the excess moisture (you can put a heavy plate or pan on top to speed this process along). Carefully cut the tofu into 1-inch cubes.

ADULTS: Heat the oil in a large, wide skillet on medium heat. Add the tofu to the pan and cook it for about 10-12 minutes, flipping the cubes over frequently with a spatula so that each piece becomes golden and a little crispy.

KIDS 6 and up: While the tofu is cooking, whisk the tamari, maple syrup, and water together in a small bowl. Make sure that the mixture is well-combined before adding it to the pan, or the maple syrup will separate from the tamari.

ADULTS: Pour the tamari mixture over the tofu, and continue to cook it until most of the sauce has been absorbed by the tofu, about 12-15 minutes. Remove the pan from the heat and transfer the tofu to a serving bowl. Many kids prefer the tofu by itself as finger food but it also goes well with grains, green salads, or in stir-fry. Store the tofu in a sealed container in the refrigerator for up to 5 days.

Kids Tips

- Kids can cut the tofu into cubes with a butter knife, but make sure that the pieces are uniform in size; otherwise they will cook unevenly.

- Kids can be in charge of draining the tofu – just make sure that they do it over the sink because it can get messy.

Cooking Tips

- Many of my students are nervous about cooking with tofu but find that once they get the hang of it, it's a very forgiving ingredient. Sautéing the tofu before adding a sauce, as in this recipe, ensures that the sauce is soaked up evenly by all the pieces.

- When sautéing tofu, it's best to use an iron skillet or non-stick pan because tofu tends to stick to stainless steel pans.

Roasted Broccoli "Trees"

Prep time: 25 minutes
Total time: 40 minutes
Serves: 2-4

G Free D Free

Ingredients

1 bunch broccoli (about 1½ pounds)

3 tablespoons olive oil

2 tablespoons toasted sesame oil

2 tablespoons all-natural maple syrup

3 tablespoons wheat-free tamari or soy sauce

2 teaspoons rice vinegar

Garnish: **sesame seeds**

Don't plan on having leftovers when you make this dish! Roasting vegetables is an easy and hands-free cooking method and creates a texture that many kids enjoy. The following cooking instructions can be used for cauliflower, carrots, bell peppers, and green beans – or a mixture of several different vegetables.

Directions

ADULTS: Preheat the oven to 425°F. Chop the broccoli florets off the stalk into medium-sized pieces. Put a steamer basket in a large, wide pot (that has a tightly-fitting lid) and fill it with a few inches of water. Arrange broccoli in the basket so that it's not overcrowded. Cover and steam the broccoli on high heat for 5-8 minutes or until it is bright green and tender – a fork should go through the thickest section easily. Do not steam it any longer than 10 minutes since you'll be cooking it again. (If you don't have a steamer, you can microwave the broccoli with 1 cup of water in a Pyrex glass dish with a tightly-fitting lid for approximately 5 minutes.)

KIDS 6 and up: While the broccoli is cooking, whisk the olive oil, toasted sesame oil, maple syrup, tamari, and rice vinegar together in a small bowl.

ADULTS: Remove the broccoli from the steamer and place it in an oven-proof pan (or keep it in the Pyrex dish if you microwaved it). Toss it with the dressing so that each broccoli piece is well-coated. Put the broccoli in the oven and roast it for 10 minutes. Remove it from the oven, stir, then roast it for an additional 5 minutes until the broccoli starts to darken and is very tender. Garnish with sesame seeds and serve immediately. Store the broccoli in a sealed container in the refrigerator for up to 3 days.

Kids Tips

- When cutting up raw broccoli, cut the outer layer of the skin off the stalks and slice the tender insides into matchsticks. These are extremely sweet and crunchy, making them a tantalizing snack for kids.

Cooking Tips

- This recipe works wonderfully with leftover cooked vegetables. Skip the steaming step, add the sauce, and roast.

- If you are preparing this dish with vegetables other than broccoli, remember to adjust the time accordingly (delicate vegetables will need less cooking time while hearty, root vegetables will need longer). If you are using several different vegetables, cut the more delicate vegetables into larger pieces and cut the thick ones smaller so that they cook at the same rate.

Cool Cuke Salad

Prep time: 20 minutes
Total time: 20 minutes
Serves: 4

G Free   D Free

Ingredients

2 teaspoons toasted sesame oil

1 tablespoon freshly squeezed lime juice
(about 1 lime)

2 tablespoons rice vinegar

1½ teaspoons granulated sugar

¼ teaspoon kosher salt or sea salt

⅛ teaspoon ground ginger

**1 English cucumber, sliced in very thin
rounds**

**1 medium-sized carrot or 6 baby carrots,
grated**

Optional: **1-2 teaspoons garlic, minced**

One of the best ways to encourage kids to embrace the concept of "salads" is to have them prepare a very simple dish with just one or two of their favorite vegetables. Since cucumbers are popular with most children, I developed this recipe based on the little salad frequently served at sushi restaurants.

Directions

KIDS 6 and up: In a medium-sized mixing bowl, whisk the toasted sesame oil, lime juice, rice vinegar, sugar, salt, and ginger together (and garlic, if using). Fold in the cucumbers and carrots. Serve immediately (or chill in the refrigerator for 30 minutes to let the flavors blend). Store the cucumber salad in a sealed container in the refrigerator for up to 3 days.

Kids Tips

- If you don't mind how the finished product looks, kids as young as 2 and 3 years old can cut the cucumbers with a butter knife, but leave the grating of carrots to older kids.

- Encourage kids to use chopsticks. It makes eating new foods a lot more fun and will improve their fine motor skills.

Cooking Tips

- This dish tastes delicious after marinating for a few hours so prepare it in advance for dinner parties.

Toasted Sesame Soba Noodles

Prep time: 30 minutes
Total time: 45 minutes
Serves: 4

D
Free

Ingredients

One 8-ounce package of soba noodles

1 tablespoon freshly squeezed lime juice
(about 1 lime)

3 tablespoons toasted sesame oil

2 tablespoons wheat-free tamari or soy sauce

2 tablespoons rice vinegar

1 tablespoon mirin

2 teaspoons all-natural maple syrup

Optional: **crushed red pepper flakes or minced fresh ginger**

½ red pepper, diced

1 medium-sized carrot or 6 baby carrots, diced

1 cup snap peas, diced

½ cup cucumber, peeled and diced

2 scallions, sliced

¼ cup cilantro, chopped

½ teaspoon kosher salt or sea salt

Freshly ground pepper to taste

Garnish with toasted sesame seeds

Optional: **avocado slices, grilled chicken or sautéed tofu**

This is one noodle dish that appeals to both food-snobs and picky eaters! Soba noodles are heartier and more nutritious than white pasta, yet very appealing to young palates. For finicky eaters, offer the scallions and cilantro in separate bowls on the table, so that each person can customize his or her own noodle salad.

Directions

ADULTS: In a medium saucepan, cook the soba noodles according to the directions on the package.

KIDS 6 and up: While the noodles are cooking, whisk the lime juice, toasted sesame oil, tamari, vinegar, mirin, maple syrup (and crushed red pepper flakes or ginger, if using) together in a small bowl.

ADULTS: Drain the noodles in a colander and run cold water over them. Transfer the noodles to a large mixing bowl.

KIDS 4 and up: Fold the red pepper, carrots, snap peas, cucumbers, scallions, and cilantro into the noodles. Add the dressing to the noodles and mix well. Season with salt and pepper. Sprinkle with sesame seeds (and top with avocado, chicken, or tofu, if using). Serve warm or chilled. This dish makes scrumptious leftovers for lunch. Store the noodle salad in a sealed container in the refrigerator for up to 5 days.

Cooking Tips

- If you are using 100% buckwheat soba noodles with no added wheat flour, make sure that you follow the cooking directions carefully because they will stick together if cooked for too long. You can add ½ cup of cold water to the boiling water two or three times throughout the cooking process in order to prevent the soba noodles from clumping together.

- If you can't eat gluten, look for gluten-free soba noodles in stores or online.

- This is the perfect dish for entertaining because it can be prepared in advance and tastes better the next day!

Kids Tips

- Take kids to a farmer's market to shop for seasonal produce, or explore an Asian supermarket for new vegetables. Just make sure that you use roughly 2 cups of vegetables in this recipe.

- Let kids pick the cilantro leaves off the stems, peel the ginger (using the tip of a spoon to scrape off the skin), and sprinkle in the sesame seeds.

Asian Veggie Rice Bowl

Prep time: 20 minutes
Total time: 50 minutes
Serves: 4

Ingredients

1 cup short- or long-grain brown rice

2 cups water

1½ cups any combination of vegetables, diced

4 baby corns, sliced

¼ cup water chestnuts, drained and halved

2 scallions, sliced

1 teaspoon kosher salt or sea salt

Freshly ground black pepper

Optional: **minced cilantro, diced avocado, tofu, mung bean sprouts, Sriracha** (spicy Asian sauce)

Dressing

3 tablespoons soy sauce

2 tablespoons toasted sesame oil

1 tablespoon mirin

2 teaspoons rice vinegar

> When we made this dish in class, it was so gratifying to see the look on parents' faces when they discovered that their kids had eaten an entire bowl of brown rice and vegetables. Again, the trick is to use toasted sesame oil and fun vegetables like baby corn and chestnuts.

Directions

ADULTS: Cook rice according to package directions. (For full instructions on how to cook brown rice, **see page 40.**) Transfer the cooked rice to a large bowl.

KIDS 4 and up: Add the vegetables, baby corn, water chestnuts, scallions, salt, and pepper to the rice and stir. Whisk the soy sauce, sesame oil, mirin, and vinegar together in a small bowl. Pour the dressing over the rice and vegetables and mix well. Add optional ingredients at this time and serve immediately. Serve the dish plain or top it with **Maple-Glazed Chicken Teriyaki (page 78)** or **Sweet-n-Sour Tofu Bites (page 68)**. Store the veggie rice bowl in a sealed container for up to 4 days. Add a little water when reheating.

Kids Tips

- Encourage kids to pick out their own vegetables or canned goods from the ethnic food section at the supermarket.

- In class, since we didn't have time to cook tofu, I'd have the kids crumble it raw (yes, it's safe to eat) directly into their rice bowls. Just make sure to drain it well first.

Cooking Tips

- Try seasonal vegetables such as leeks, spring onions, peas, summer squash, eggplant, or squash.

- If you're trying to eat more rice, it's worth investing in a rice cooker. There are many inexpensive models on the market.

Maple-Glazed Chicken Teriyaki

Prep time: 15 minutes
Total time: 45 minutes
Serves: 4

G Free   D Free

Ingredients

2 boneless, skinless chicken breast cutlets

¼ cup wheat-free tamari or soy sauce

2 tablespoons all-natural maple syrup

½ teaspoon garlic, minced (about 1 garlic clove)

1-2 tablespoons vegetable oil

Optional: **add minced fresh ginger to the marinade and garnish with toasted cashews and scallions**

This is a fast, inexpensive dinner that the entire family will enjoy. You can start marinating the chicken the night before or in the morning so that it will take just minutes to prepare after you get home from a long day. Feel free to experiment with different flavors in the marinade – try adding fresh herbs, vinegars, or dried spices.

Directions

KIDS 8 and up: If the chicken breasts are really thick, cover them with plastic wrap (to prevent splattering) and pound them gently with a meat tenderizer until each breast is about ½-inch thick.

KIDS 6 and up: In a small bowl, whisk the soy sauce, maple syrup and garlic together (and ginger, if using).

KIDS 8 and up: Cut the chicken into 2-inch square pieces. Put the chicken in an 8-inch by 8-inch dish and pour the sauce over it. Move them around to coat each piece well. Cover the dish with plastic wrap and allow the chicken to marinate in the refrigerator for at least 15 minutes or overnight (up to 24 hours).

ADULTS: Heat the oil in a wide, deep skillet over medium heat. Using a slotted spoon or a fork, add the chicken to the pan without the marinade (so that the chicken will get crispy). Set the remaining marinade aside. Cook the chicken for 5-7 minutes and then turn over each piece. Continue to cook for another 5-7 minutes. Turn the pieces over until they're browned and thoroughly cooked on both sides. Cook for a total of about 10 minutes (but not more than 15 minutes). Add the remaining marinade, turn the heat down to low, and cook for just a minute or two longer until most of the marinade is absorbed. Remove the pan from the heat.

To determine if the chicken is fully cooked, cut the largest piece open to see if the center is fully white (and not pink). Serve over plain rice or with the **Asian Veggie Rice Bowl (page 76)** and garnish with nuts and scallions, if using. Store the chicken in a sealed container in the refrigerator for up to 2-3 days.

Kids Tips

- Anyone who handles raw chicken must wash his or her hands extremely well afterwards!

- If you don't have a meat tenderizer, you can use a rolling pin or any other heavy kitchen tool to pound the chicken.

Cooking Tips

- Remember to use a plastic or glass cutting board rather than a wooden cutting board, which can absorb the bacteria from the raw chicken. For more information about preventing cross-contamination, **see page 6**.

Marvelous Mushroom Potstickers

Prep time: 1 hour
Total time: 1¼ hours
Yields: 50 potstickers
Serves: 4-6

Ingredients

1 pound button or cremini mushrooms
(about 40 mushrooms)

1 tablespoon olive oil

1 small yellow onion, finely diced

2-3 teaspoons garlic, minced

2 teaspoons fresh ginger, minced
(or 1 teaspoon ground ginger)

1 tablespoon mirin

1 tablespoon rice vinegar

3 scallions, sliced

1 tablespoon chives

½ teaspoon kosher salt or sea salt

Freshly ground pepper to taste

Optional: **8 ounces firm tofu, drained and crumbled
or 1 cup cooked chicken, finely chopped**

40-50 round dumpling wrappers

¼-½ cup vegetable oil for pan-frying

> Potstickers are a meal and an art project wrapped into one! They take a little while to prepare but kids are usually happy to do the majority of the work. They taste so good that it's worth it in the end. Save this recipe for a leisurely, rainy afternoon when the kids have plenty of time to get creative and design different shapes.

Directions

Kids 4 and up: Clean the mushrooms by wiping them with a damp paper towel. Slice or dice them and set them aside.

ADULTS: Heat the olive oil in a large, deep skillet. Sauté the onions for 10-15 minutes or until they are translucent. Add the garlic, ginger and mushrooms and cook for about 10 more minutes. (If you are using tofu, add it to the pan now. Move the other ingredients to the sides so that the tofu can cook for 8-10 minutes or until golden.)

Drizzle the mirin and rice vinegar over the mushroom mixture and stir. Add the scallions, chives, salt and pepper and cook for a few more minutes. Turn off the heat. (If you are adding cooked chicken, put it in now and combine with the rest of the ingredients.) Allow the mixture to cool enough to handle it with bare fingers. You can store the mushroom mixture in a sealed container in the refrigerator for up to 2 days before preparing the potstickers.

KIDS 6 and up: Line a baking sheet with wax paper to prevent the wrappers from sticking. Set out a small bowl of water. Place 1 heaping teaspoon of the mushroom mixture in the center of each dumpling wrapper. Dab the outer edges of the wrapper with water. Bring the edges together to form a half-moon (or whatever shape you'd like) and carefully fold and press to seal. Make sure that the edges are sealed well.

Place potstickers on the baking sheet and cover them loosely with a damp dish towel so that they don't dry out while you continue assembling the rest until there is no more filling. At this point, you can cover them tightly with plastic wrap and refrigerate up to 24 hours, or freeze.

ADULTS: In a large, heavy skillet, heat about ¼ cup of oil. Add one potsticker to the pan to see if the oil sizzles – if it does, add the rest but be careful not to overcrowd the pan. When the bottoms are golden-brown, after about 3-5 minutes, flip them over so that each side gets crispy. Add more oil as needed. Store the potstickers in a sealed container in the refrigerator for up to 3 days.

Kids Tips

- Make sure kids do not overstuff the potstickers and that they seal the edges really well.

Cooking Tips

- **See page 68** for instructions on how to drain tofu.

- Instead of preparing the filling from scratch, you can use up leftover cooked vegetables or chicken instead.

Soy Scallion Dipping Sauce

Prep time: 10 minutes
Total time: 10 minutes
Serves: 6

D
Free

Ingredients

5 tablespoons wheat-free tamari or soy sauce

1 tablespoon rice vinegar

1 tablespoon scallions, minced

½ teaspoon garlic, minced (about 1 small clove)

2 teaspoons honey

Directions

KIDS 2 and up: Combine all the ingredients in a bowl and mix well. Serve immediately or, to allow the flavors to blend, prepare the sauce 30 minutes prior to serving.

Nutrition 101

Kids who eat balanced meals are more likely to sleep better, do well in school, have the energy to be physically active, and less likely to have meltdowns. Make sure that your kids eat protein in the morning and throughout the day in order to keep their blood sugar balanced and their moods even-keel.

Teach your kids that their growing bodies need all three macronutrients (protein, carbohydrates, and fats), as well as fiber, from quality sources.

Protein Sources

Beef, poultry, fish, eggs, dairy, beans, nuts, nut butters, seeds, and whole grains.

Carbohydrate Sources

Vegetables, fruit, and whole grains. Try to limit processed, white carbohydrate products and stick to whole foods as much as possible.

Fat Sources

"Good" fats are found in avocados, nuts, seeds, oils, sardines, mackerel, and wild salmon (farm-raised fish are not a good source of omega-3 fatty acids). Limit saturated fats and avoid hydrogenated oils, which are the harmful trans fats.

Fiber Sources

Fiber plays an important role in disease prevention - it can be found in vegetables, fruits, nuts, seeds, beans, and whole grains.

Notes

Pretty much all the honest truth-telling there is in the world is done by children.

Oliver Wendell Holmes

Chapter 9

Mouthwatering Mediterranean Meals

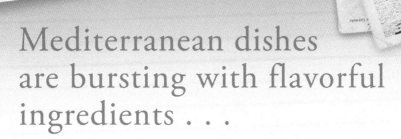

Mediterranean dishes are bursting with flavorful ingredients . . .

. . . that are healthy and kid-friendly, including chickpeas, sesame tahini, tomatoes, cucumbers, spinach, and couscous.

Crispy Pita Chips

Prep time: 10 minutes
Total time: 25 minutes
Yields: 32 chips

D Free

Ingredients

2 whole-wheat or white pita pockets

3 tablespoons olive oil

Kosher salt or sea salt to taste

Optional: **minced garlic or dried herbs such as oregano, basil, parsley**

My students adored this recipe so much that we made it several times each semester. Pita chips take only minutes to make, but if you serve them at dinner parties, guests will treat them like a gourmet dish you've spent hours preparing.

Directions

ADULTS: Preheat the oven to 350°F degrees.

KIDS 8 and up: On a cutting board, carefully slice each pita into eight triangle-shapes with a pizza cutter or a knife. Pull each triangle in half so that one pita pocket will yield a total of 16 pieces. Lay the pita pieces close together on a greased baking sheet (or one lined with parchment paper). Pour the olive oil into a small bowl.

KIDS 2 and up: Brush each piece of pita generously with olive oil using a pastry brush. Sprinkle with salt (and herbs and garlic, if using).

ADULTS: Bake the chips for 12-14 minutes, or until crispy and golden-brown around the edges. Store the pita chips in a sealed container or bag at room temperature for up to 4 days.

Kids Tips

- The pizza cutter is a popular tool with children but smaller kids need close supervision when using it. Alternatively, kids can cut the pita bread with a plastic knife or an adult can use a chef's knife.

- Many kids go a little overboard when adding herbs and salt so make sure that they don't add too much!

Cooking Tips

- Try to purchase pita bread that does not contain any hydrogenated oils (which are the harmful trans-fats).

Tangy Tzatziki
(Cucumber and Yogurt Dip)

Prep time: 20 minutes
Total time: 20 minutes
Yields: 2 cups

G
Free

Ingredients

**1 cup plain whole milk yogurt
or Greek yogurt**

½ cup sour cream

½ English cucumber, grated (about 1 cup)

1 tablespoon apple cider vinegar

2 tablespoons freshly squeezed lemon juice
(about 1 lemon)

1 tablespoon olive oil

1 teaspoon garlic, minced (about 1 clove)

2 teaspoons fresh dill, chopped
(or 1 teaspoon dried)

½ teaspoon kosher salt or sea salt

Freshly ground pepper to taste

If kids can dip it, they'll eat it! This kid-friendly dish tastes better the longer it marinates, so plan on serving it as an after-school snack all week long. Traditional tzatziki calls for draining the yogurt and cucumber for at least half an hour but this is a much quicker recipe and turns out just as tasty.

Directions

KIDS 6 and up: Drain the yogurt of excess liquid by carefully tipping the container over the sink. Scoop the yogurt into a medium-sized bowl, add the sour cream, and stir.

KIDS 2 and up: Gather the grated cucumber into your fists and squeeze out as much liquid as you can until it's drained of moisture. Add the cucumber to the yogurt and sour cream mixture. Stir in the vinegar, lemon juice, olive oil, garlic, dill, salt, and pepper and combine well. Serve immediately at room temperature with **Crispy Pita Chips (page 86)** or marinate in the refrigerator for a few hours so that the flavors blend.

Kids Tips

- Kids get a kick out of squeezing water from the cucumber, but it can get a little messy. Make sure they do it over the sink or in a large bowl with dish towels nearby.

Cooking Tips

- I recommend cooking with whole milk yogurt, or at the very least, low-fat. Nonfat yogurt doesn't work as well for creamy dishes and often contains added sugars and preservatives.

- For a light, everyday snack for kids, I replace the sour cream with ½ cup of yogurt. For a dinner party, however, I recommend using sour cream to create a richer dish.

Roasted Red Pepper Hummus

Prep time: 20 minutes
(plus roasting pepper)
Total time: 1 hour
Serves: 6-8

G Free   D Free

Ingredients

One 15-ounce can chickpeas (or 2 cups cooked)

1 large roasted red pepper (about ½ cup)

3 tablespoons parsley, chopped

3-4 tablespoons freshly squeezed lemon juice (about 2 lemons)

1 tablespoon freshly squeezed lime juice (about 1 lime)

2-3 teaspoons garlic, minced (about 2-3 cloves)

2 tablespoons olive oil

½ cup sesame tahini

1 teaspoon kosher salt or sea salt

Optional: **4 ounces silken tofu, well-drained**

> Hummus and other bean dips are ideal dishes for kids who don't eat a lot of protein. In class, my students mash the chickpeas with a fork instead of using a food processor, which is a lot easier than it sounds!

Directions

KIDS 8 and up: Clean off the top of the canned beans. Open the can and drain the liquid. Rinse the beans off in a colander and drain well. For instructions on how to roast peppers, see next page.

ADULTS with KIDS: Blend the roasted pepper, beans, parsley, 3 tablespoons of lemon juice, lime juice, garlic, olive oil, tahini, and salt (and tofu, if using) in a food processor until desired consistency is achieved (some people like it chunky while others prefer it very smooth). If there is any excess oil from the roasted pepper, add it now. Feel free to add more garlic, lemon juice, olive oil, or salt according to taste.

Garnish with slices of red pepper. Serve hummus warm or chilled with **Crispy Pita Chips (page 86)** and vegetable sticks. This dish keeps for a week in an airtight container in the refrigerator.

Kids Tips

- If you don't have a food processor, kids can mash the chickpeas with a fork in a large bowl. Keep some extra beans on hand because they tend to eat them while they work.

- Adding tofu to this dish is an ideal way to double the protein without changing the flavor.

Cooking Tips

- **Roasting peppers:** There are two methods – you can char peppers over a flame using tongs or roast them in the oven by preheating the oven to broil. Make sure that the top rack is positioned so that the pepper will be 4-5 inches away from the top of the oven. Place the pepper on a baking sheet lined with foil. Roast it until it is black and charred, for about 40 minutes, flipping it occasionally with tongs. Remove it from the oven, close it up in a paper bag or put it in a metal bowl and cover with plastic wrap in order to loosen the skin. When the pepper has cooled, peel the skin, and remove the seeds. Discard the peel and seeds, but save the oil released from the pepper. Cut 2 or 3 slices for garnish and use the rest for the hummus.

- For plain hummus, omit the red pepper and add in some extra olive oil to ensure that the dish turns out creamy.

- If you prepare the beans from scratch, you'll appreciate the difference in taste. **See page 25** for instructions on how to cook beans.

Whipped Tahini Sauce

Prep time: 20 minutes
Total time: 20 minutes
Serves: 6

Ingredients

1 cup sesame tahini (raw or roasted)

4 tablespoons freshly squeezed lemon juice (about 2 lemons)

2 tablespoons freshly squeezed lime juice (about 2 limes)

1-2 teaspoons garlic, minced (about 2 cloves)

1 tablespoon parsley, chopped

1 tablespoon olive oil

¼ teaspoon kosher salt or sea salt

½-¾ cup water

Garnish: **1 teaspoon parsley, minced**

When I worked on a kibbutz in Israel, we prepared this dish almost every day and ate it with our salads at breakfast and dinner. Tahini is perfect for kids because it has a mild flavor and a texture similar to nut butters. Transform any entrée or side dish into a Mediterranean feast by adding this creamy sauce.

Directions

KIDS with ADULT: Purée the tahini, lemon juice, lime juice, garlic, parsley, oil, and salt in a food processor or a blender. Slowly drizzle in only ½ cup of water, blend again, and then check the consistency. For a thinner sauce, add in more water, 1 tablespoon at a time, (and/or more lemon juice) until it is the desired consistency. Transfer it to a serving dish and garnish with parsley.

This sauce can be served with the **Fantastic Falafel Pita Pockets (see page 98)** or **Light-n-Lemony Quinoa Tabouli (page 102)** or, as a dressing over vegetables, rice, tofu, or chicken. Store the sauce in a sealed container in the refrigerator for up to a week.

Kids Tips

- After the kids juice the lemons and lime, give them the citrus fruits to chew on.

Cooking Tips

- To turn the sauce into a dip, simply use less water. Salad lovers can thin it out by adding more lemon juice or water to create a light, lemony dressing.

- This dish is a great opportunity to add in flax oil for extra omega-3 fatty acids. Because flax oil is very fragile, buy only small amounts, keep it in the refrigerator, and never heat it.

The Ultimate Greek Salad

Prep time: 30 minutes
Total time: 30 minutes
Serves: 6

G
Free

Ingredients

2 on-the-vine or plum tomatoes, diced

1½ English cucumbers, diced

1 red pepper, finely diced

3 tablespoons red onion, finely diced

1 cup pitted kalamata olives, whole or halved

1-2 tablespoons parsley, chopped

Dressing

3 tablespoons red wine vinegar

2 teaspoons Dijon mustard

2 teaspoons honey

1 teaspoon dried Italian Seasoning

½ teaspoon kosher salt or sea salt

Freshly ground black pepper

¼ cup olive oil

Garnish: ¾ cup feta cheese and
1 tablespoon parsley

When one of my students took her first bite of this salad, she exclaimed, "This is so good, it makes me want to dance!" Often, the parents of my students are disappointed that they do not have the opportunity to try this dish because their kids devour it first.

Directions

KIDS 2 and up: In a large bowl, combine the tomatoes, cucumber, red pepper, and red onion. Gently fold in the olives and parsley and stir.

KIDS 6 and up: In a separate bowl, whisk the red wine vinegar, Dijon mustard, honey, dried herbs, salt and pepper together. While whisking continuously, slowly add the oil.

KIDS 2 and up: Pour the dressing over the vegetables and toss to blend. Crumble the feta cheese over the top of the salad, garnish with parsley, and serve. Store the Greek salad in a sealed container in the refrigerator for up to 2 days.

Kids Tips

- When introducing salad dressings to children, I add more honey and less vinegar to ease them into strong flavors.

- Buy extra produce because kids will often end up eating a good portion of the vegetables while they are chopping them.

- For finicky eaters, omit the red onion and swap the kalamata olives and feta for black olives and a mild white cheese.

- If kids are in charge of whisking the dressing, use a large bowl for less of a mess!

Cooking Tips

- Arrange the ingredients like a salad bar so that each family member can customize his or her own dish.

- Turn this salad into a full meal by adding grilled chicken strips or hard-boiled eggs.

- Italian Seasoning is a mixture of basil, oregano, thyme, marjoram and other herbs.

Mini Spinach Pies

Prep time: 40 minutes
Total time: 1 hour
Yields: 18 mini pies

Ingredients

One 10-ounce box or bag of frozen spinach, thawed and drained

4 eggs

One 15-ounce container ricotta cheese

2½-3 cups Cheddar cheese, grated

¼ cup grated Parmesan cheese

¼ teaspoon ground nutmeg

1½ teaspoons kosher salt or sea salt

Freshly ground pepper to taste

Cooking spray or olive oil mister

Two sheets of puff pastry, chilled

This dish always gets the kids jumping out of their seats with excitement. I discovered that kids will eat just about anything if it's inside puff pastry! The first time I made these with my nephew, he loved them so much that he insisted we make a second batch for his school lunches.

Directions

ADULTS: Preheat the oven to 350°F. For instructions on how to thaw and drain spinach, **see page 35**.

KIDS 4 and up: In a large bowl, beat the eggs and stir in the ricotta cheese. Add the Cheddar cheese, Parmesan cheese, spinach, nutmeg, salt, and pepper, and stir together. Grease or spray two standard 12-cup muffin pans.

KIDS 6 and up: On a dry surface, lay one of the puff pastry sheets flat (keep the other one in the refrigerator until you need it). Cut the sheet into 9 even squares. Use a rolling pin or your fingers to make each square a little larger but still maintain the square shape. Carefully insert each one into the muffin pan, so that the dough covers the sides of the muffin cup. It's okay if the corners stick out – the pastry will puff up in the oven. Divide the cheese filling evenly among the pastry cups, filling each one to the top.

ADULTS: Bake the pies for 20-22 minutes. The filling should be set and the pastry crust should be puffed up and golden. Serve warm or at room temperature. Store the pies in a sealed container in the refrigerator for 2-3 days or in the freezer for up to 6 months.

Cooking Tips

- You can usually find puff pastry in the freezer section at major grocery stores. One box typically contains 2 sheets. Try to find puff pastry made without trans-fats.

- Take the puff pastry out of the freezer and thaw it in the refrigerator for at least 4 hours (or up to 1 day) before using it. It's important to keep it in the refrigerator until right before you use it.

Thank you, Megan Brenn-White, for inspiring this recipe!

Kids Tips

- This dish works well for on-the-go breakfasts and school lunches because it travels well and can be eaten at room temperature without utensils.

- Kids as young as 2 years old can master how to break an egg. **See page 8** for instructions on how to teach **Breaking an Egg.**

Fantastic Falafel Pita Pockets

Prep time: 1 hour
Total time: 1 hour (plus baking potato)
Yields: 20 small patties

D Free

Ingredients

¾ cup baked potato (about 1 small russet potato)

One 15-ounce can chickpeas (or 2 cups cooked)

1-2 teaspoons garlic, minced (about 2 cloves)

2 tablespoons parsley, minced

1 teaspoon celery seed

1 teaspoon ground coriander

¼-½ teaspoon cumin

1 tablespoon unbleached all-purpose flour

1 tablespoon breadcrumbs

1 tablespoon olive oil

½ teaspoon baking powder

½ teaspoon kosher salt or sea salt

Freshly ground black pepper

3-4 tablespoons vegetable oil for pan-frying

6 to 8 pita pockets

½ English cucumber, peeled and cubed

2 on-the-vine or plum tomatoes, cubed

Falafel, a savory Middle Eastern street food, is a fried patty made of ground chickpeas. To make this dish healthier and more kid-friendly, I replaced the onions with a baked potato and pan-fried the falafel instead of deep-frying it. Every time I tested this recipe, my nephew gobbled up the entire batch, straight out of the fridge.

Directions

KIDS 6 and up: Peel the potato after it has cooled and discard the skin. For instructions on how to cook beans from scratch, **see page 25**.

KIDS with ADULTS: In a food processor, purée the potato with the chickpeas, garlic, parsley, celery seed, coriander, and cumin. Add the flour, breadcrumbs, oil, baking powder, salt, and pepper and blend for another minute. Check the mixture to make sure it binds together well – it

should be moist but not sticky. If it's too dry, add a little more olive oil. If it's too wet, add a small amount of breadcrumbs.

KIDS 6 and up: Roll the batter into small, 1½-inch patties, flatten slightly, and put them on a plate near the stove.

ADULTS: Coat the bottom of a heavy skillet with 2 tablespoons of vegetable oil and heat it over medium heat. Add one patty to the pan to see if the oil sizzles – if it does, add more but be careful not to overcrowd the pan. Cook the patties for 4-5 minutes, turning them occasionally, until both sides are brown and crispy, a total of 7-10 minutes. Transfer them to a plate. Slice the top part of the pita pocket off so that it's easier to insert food. Serve the falafel inside pita pockets with diced cucumber, tomatoes, and **Whipped Tahini Sauce (page 92)** drizzled on top. Store the patties in a sealed container in the refrigerator for up to 5 days.

Cooking Tips

- **Baking potatoes:** Rinse and scrub the potato, puncture it several times with a fork, and bake it on a pan or inside foil at 375°F for about 35-40 minutes or until it is very tender. You can also microwave it on high until it is soft. Allow it to cool.

- Make sure the oil is very hot the entire time you are cooking the patties so that they maintain their shape and become crispy. The oil should sizzle when you add each new patty.

- If you want a lighter version of this dish, put patties on a greased baking sheet (or one lined with parchment paper) and bake for 12 minutes at 350°F. Remove the baking sheet from the oven, flip each patty, and bake for another 10 minutes.

Kids Tips

- If you don't have a food processor, kids can mash the potato and beans by hand. Stir in the rest of the ingredients.

- If kids are uninterested in eating the falafel inside the pita pocket with vegetables, they can dip the patties into the **Whipped Tahini Sauce (page 92)** instead.

Rainbow Couscous Salad

Prep time: 30 minutes
Total time: 40 minutes
Serves: 4-6

D Free

Ingredients

One 10- or 12-ounce box of plain couscous

2 cups any combination of vegetables, diced

3-4 scallions, sliced

¼ cup currants or dried cranberries

½ cup fresh parsley, chopped

¼ cup fresh mint, chopped

Optional: **beans, nuts, feta cheese, cooked chicken or shrimp**

Dressing

1 tablespoon white wine vinegar

1 tablespoon freshly squeezed lemon juice (about ½ lemon)

2-3 teaspoons garlic, minced (about 3 cloves)

2 teaspoons white miso

1 teaspoon celery seed

½ teaspoon dried oregano

½ teaspoon freshly ground black pepper

1-2 tablespoons of honey

½ cup olive oil

A couscous medley is the perfect dinner for chaotic weeknights since it takes only minutes to prepare and you can add in leftover vegetables or meat from the night before. It's also convenient for lunch boxes since it can be served at room temperature.

Directions

ADULTS: Cook the couscous according to package directions.

KIDS 4 and up: Add the diced vegetables, scallions, and dried fruit to the couscous and stir. Gently fold in the parsley and mint (and the optional ingredients, if using).

KIDS 6 and up: In a small bowl, whisk the vinegar, lemon juice, garlic, miso, celery seed, oregano, black pepper, and honey together and slowly add in the olive oil. Pour the dressing over the couscous and vegetables and stir. Serve this dish cold or warm. Store the couscous in a sealed container in the refrigerator for up to 5 days.

Kids Tips

- Since this dish can be easily changed according to taste, encourage kids to come up with their own dressing and combination of vegetables.

Cooking Tips

- Suggested vegetables and other dried fruit options: carrots, celery, radishes, mushrooms, spring onions, leeks, artichokes, raisins, or chopped apricots.

- Try adding seasonal vegetables, such as sautéed leafy greens in the winter, roasted beets in the spring, or peas in the summer.

- Miso is a fermented product like vinegar so it can be stored in your fridge indefinitely. It should not be heated. I recommend white miso because of its mild, kid-friendly flavor, but you can use any kind of miso. (Or, omit it if you don't have it on hand.) Most health food stores carry several different flavors so feel free to experiment.

Light-n-Lemony Quinoa Tabouli

Prep time: 20 minutes
Total time: 40 minutes
Serves: 4-6

Ingredients

1 cup quinoa

2 cups water

¼ cup mint, chopped

½ cup parsley, chopped

3-4 on-the-vine or plum tomatoes, diced

3 scallions, sliced

¼ teaspoon celery seed

¼ cup freshly squeezed lemon juice (about 2 lemons)

3 tablespoons olive oil

Kosher salt or sea salt to taste

Freshly ground black pepper

Optional: **extra mint or parsley, cumin, crushed red pepper flakes, or sautéed eggplant**

This delightful salad is made with quinoa (pronounced KEEN-wa) rather than bulgur, the traditional grain used in tabouli. Quinoa is high in protein, cooks in only 20 minutes, and is ideal for kids because of its light and fluffy texture. Experiment with this recipe by using Mexican spices for a Latin theme or throwing in some basil and mozzarella if you want to serve it with an Italian meal.

Directions

ADULTS: Cook quinoa according to package directions (or follow the same instructions for cooking brown rice found on **page 40** except that you cook quinoa for a total of 20 minutes).

KIDS 4 and up: Fluff the cooked quinoa with a fork and transfer it to a medium-sized bowl. Add the mint, parsley, tomatoes, scallions, and celery seed to the quinoa and stir. In a small bowl, whisk the lemon juice and olive oil together. Pour the dressing over the mixture and toss well. Season with salt and pepper and serve immediately. Store the tabouli in a sealed container in the refrigerator for up to 5 days.

Kids Tips

- Since quinoa is very absorbent, it will take on any flavor, so encourage kids to explore different fresh herbs, spices, or vegetables when preparing this dish.

Cooking Tips

- Unless the quinoa package says that it is "pre-rinsed," you'll need to rinse it with water in a fine-meshed strainer in order to remove the saponin (a natural bitter coating).

- For extra flavor, try cooking the quinoa in chicken or vegetable stock instead of water.

Notes

Even when freshly washed and relieved of all obvious confections, children tend to be sticky.

Fran Lebowitz

Chapter 10

Delectable Desserts

Baking is a great way for young children . . .

. . . to start working in the kitchen. Most of these dessert recipes include at least one nutritious ingredient, such as fruit, oats, or yogurt.

Heavenly Banana Ice Cream

Prep time: 10 minutes (plus 1 day for freezing)
Total time: 10 minutes
Serves: 3-4

G Free   D Free

Ingredients

3 bananas

¾-1 cup of milk, soy milk, coconut milk, or apple juice

Optional toppings: **mini chocolate chips, toasted nuts, sliced strawberries, or shredded coconut**

This is, by far, one of the most popular recipes that I've ever taught. At the end of class, I prepare this treat for my small students and they quickly gobble it up. It's a guilt-free indulgence because it's made entirely with bananas and milk or juice.

Directions

KIDS 2 and up: Peel bananas and break them into 2-inch pieces. Put them in a ziptop bag and freeze for at least 24 hours or up to several months. Take the bananas out of the freezer and let them thaw for 2-3 minutes.

KIDS with ADULT: Put the bananas and ½ cup of your chosen liquid into a food processor (or blender) and purée for a couple of minutes. Add another ¼ cup of liquid and purée.

ADULTS: Every 1-2 minutes, use a spatula to adjust the bananas when they get stuck in the blade. If necessary, add the final ¼ cup of liquid. This dish does not keep well so it must be eaten immediately. Serve plain or with toppings.

Kids Tips

- To include the kids in the preparation, have them stand on a stool to press the food processor buttons and help assess when the banana ice cream needs more liquid.

- Once the food processor blade is safely removed and out of reach, the kids can help scoop out the banana ice cream with a spatula and garnish each serving with toppings.

Cooking Tips

- This dish can be made in a blender but it's much easier to prepare it in the wide bowl of a food processor.

- You may need to adjust the liquid every time you make this dish because bananas vary in size. Go easy when adding the liquid – you can always add more. Eventually the mixture will begin to look like soft ice cream.

- If your freezer runs on the colder side, you may want to allow the bananas to thaw a little longer than 2-3 minutes. Just use caution, because the longer they thaw out, the less the final product looks like ice cream.

Vanilla Crispie Bars

Prep time: 20 minutes
Total time: 20 minutes
(plus 1 hour for hardening)
Yields: 16 squares

Ingredients

2 teaspoons butter or cooking spray

4 cups puffed rice cereal

1½ cups quick-cooking rolled oats

½ cup white chocolate chips

4 tablespoons butter (½ stick)

1 tablespoon vanilla extract

1 cup brown rice syrup

1 tablespoon corn syrup

½ teaspoon kosher salt or sea salt

2 teaspoons butter or cooking spray

Garnish: **¼ cup white chocolate chips**

This is an updated version of the classic krispie treats but with better-quality ingredients such as oats and brown rice syrup, which doesn't spike blood sugar as much as refined sugars do. Forewarning: this recipe is very addictive. Everyone has trouble eating just one square – including myself!

Directions

KIDS 6 and up: Grease an 8-inch by 8-inch pan with butter or cooking spray.

KIDS 2 and up: In a large bowl, mix the puffed rice cereal, rolled oats and ½ cup of white chocolate chips.

ADULTS: In a wide saucepan, heat the butter on medium-low heat until melted (being careful not to burn it). Add the vanilla, brown rice syrup, corn syrup, and salt, and cook until the mixture bubbles. Stir it together and cook for 2-3 minutes. Remove the pan from the heat. Add the puffed rice, oats, and white chocolate chips to the butter mixture. Stir everything together and transfer it to the greased 8-inch by 8-inch pan.

KIDS 8 and up: When the mixture is cool enough to touch, spread it evenly throughout the pan using a spatula or your fingers. Press the mixture down well so that it can be cut into bars once it hardens. Garnish it with white chocolate chips by gently pressing them into the puffed rice mixture. Leave the pan at room temperature for at least 1 hour so that it will harden.

ADULTS: Cut the crispies into squares and serve. Store the extra bars in a sealed container at room temperature for up to 5 days.

Kids Tips

- If your kids are on a gluten-free diet, use gluten-free oats and puffed rice cereal.

Cooking Tips

- Brown rice syrup is a natural sweetener that can be found at most health food stores.

- You can replace the white chocolate chips with regular chocolate chips, raisins or nuts. But don't use more than ¾ cup total of the alternate ingredients or the mixture won't stick together.

Very Berry and Creamsicle Smoothies

Prep time: 5 minutes
Total time: 5 minutes
Serves: 3-4

Ingredients

Very Berry Smoothies

2 cups vanilla yogurt

¾ cup orange juice

2 medium bananas, peeled and broken into large pieces

1 cup frozen strawberries OR ¾ cup frozen blueberries

For Creamsicle Smoothies: use 1 cup of ice instead of frozen berries

Smoothies are a superb snack and a great breakfast because they contain nutrient-dense ingredients like fruit and yogurt. If you have trouble getting your kids to eat breakfast, just whip this up the night before, store it in the fridge, and pour it into a to-go cup in the morning.

Directions

KIDS with ADULT: Add all the ingredients to a blender and purée until very smooth. Serve immediately or store in the refrigerator for up to two days.

Cooking Tips

- You can use fresh berries when they are in season. Just make sure that you add a frozen ingredient such as ice or a frozen banana, so that the smoothie will become frothy like a milkshake.

- Replace the orange juice with pineapple juice for a tropical version.

- It's best to avoid non-fat yogurts since they often contain added sugars. Instead, use low-fat or whole milk yogurt for this recipe.

Chocolate-Dipped Strawberries

Prep time: 20 minutes
Total time: 20 minutes
(plus 1 hour for hardening)
Yields: 30 strawberries

Ingredients

30 medium-sized strawberries

6 ounces of semi-sweet chocolate

1 tablespoon unsalted butter

1 tablespoon corn syrup

Dipping food into melted chocolate is always an exciting activity! When making this recipe with kids, make sure that you keep the chocolate cool enough for their little fingers to touch but not so cold that it hardens. Dip other fruits, pretzels, or graham crackers into the chocolate and make your own Fondue Party!

Directions

KIDS 2 and up: Wash and dry the strawberries. Make sure that the berries are completely dry or the chocolate will not adhere to them. Line a baking sheet with waxed paper.

ADULTS: In the top of a double boiler that you've set over simmering water, stir the chocolate, butter, and corn syrup until the chocolate melts and the mixture is smooth. Remove the chocolate from the heat but leave the water simmering in case the chocolate starts to harden and you need to re-heat it. If you're worried about small kids touching a still-warm pan, you can transfer the chocolate to a cool dish.

KIDS 2 and up: Hold each strawberry by its stem and dip it ¾ of the way into the chocolate. Swirl it and shake off excess chocolate. Place the chocolate-dipped strawberry on the baking sheet lined with waxed paper and repeat with the rest of the strawberries. They can harden in the refrigerator or at room temperature.

Kids Tips

- If your kids want to create designs, melt some white chocolate, dip a spoon in, and swirl designs onto the chocolate-dipped strawberries. Or, they can dip the chocolate-dipped strawberries in sprinkles before the chocolate hardens.

Cooking Tips

- It's best if the strawberries are at room temperature rather than cold.

- If you don't have a double boiler (which is necessary since the chocolate will burn if put directly over heat), simply place a metal bowl on top of a saucepan or put a small saucepan inside another larger saucepan. Alternatively, you can microwave the chocolate, butter, and corn syrup in a microwave-safe bowl in 30-second intervals until it is melted.

- "Simmering" means a few small bubbles are barely breaking the surface.

- This recipe can be prepared up to 1-2 days before serving – just store the strawberries in the refrigerator and remove 30 minutes before serving.

Mini Chocolate Chip Blondies

Prep time: 20 minutes
Total time: 40 minutes
Yields: 12-16 bars

Ingredients

2 teaspoons butter or cooking spray

½ cup unsalted butter, softened (1 stick)

¾ cup granulated sugar

¾ cup brown sugar, packed

2 eggs

1 teaspoon vanilla extract

2¼ cups unbleached, all-purpose flour

½ teaspoon sea salt

1 teaspoon baking soda

1⅓ cups chocolate chips (or raisins or peanut butter chips)

My cousin Sonya, baker extraordinaire, developed this low-fat recipe years ago as a potluck dessert that she could make in a rush. My students tell me that when they serve these blondies at dinner parties, their guests beg for the recipe.

Directions

ADULTS: Preheat the oven to 375°F.

KIDS 6 and up: Grease an 8-inch by 8-inch baking pan with butter or cooking spray.

KIDS with ADULT: In the bowl of an electric mixer fitted with the paddle attachment, beat the butter and white sugar on medium speed until light and fluffy. Add the brown sugar, eggs and vanilla extract and mix until the batter is creamy. Scrape down the sides of the bowl as needed. In a separate medium-sized bowl, combine the flour, salt and baking soda.

While the mixer is on low, add the flour mixture gradually and blend together until all the ingredients are thoroughly combined. Add the chocolate chips and mix together for just 1 minute. The dough will be very stiff. Using a spatula, spread the cookie dough batter evenly throughout the baking pan.

ADULTS: Bake for 18-20 minutes or until golden brown and a toothpick inserted in the center comes out clean. Allow the blondies to cool for at least 30 minutes before cutting them into squares. Serve blondies immediately, store them in a sealed container at room temperature for up to 2 days, or freeze them in a ziptop bag for up to 3-6 months.

Kids Tips

- Kids as young as 2 years old can master how to break an egg. **See page 8** for instructions on how to teach **Breaking an Egg.**

Cooking Tips

- If you want to make traditional cookies instead of blondies, drop small balls of dough onto a greased baking sheet (or one lined with parchment paper). Bake them for 8-11 minutes or until golden brown around the edges. Leave the cookies on the pan for 5 minutes before transferring them to a cooling rack.

- If you don't have a standing electric mixer, use a hand-mixer.

Recipe adapted from Sonya Jassen Basseri

Apple Carrot Muffins

Prep time: 25 minutes
Total time: 50 minutes
Yields: 12 muffins or 32 mini muffins

Ingredients

1 cup whole-wheat flour

1 cup unbleached, all-purpose flour

1 tablespoon baking powder

¼ teaspoon sea salt

½ teaspoon cinnamon

3 eggs

½ cup granulated sugar

½ cup vegetable oil

1 cup apple, peeled and grated (about 1 apple)

1 cup carrot, peeled and grated (about 1 carrot)

These muffins are fluffy, sweet, and packed with wholesome ingredients including apples, carrots and whole-wheat flour. Kids can help prepare the entire dish since it doesn't require an electric mixer. These muffins are a perfect treat for school parties or potlucks because they are easy to transport and everyone loves them!

Directions

ADULTS: Preheat the oven to 350°F.

KIDS 2 and up: In a large bowl, mix the flours, baking powder, salt, and cinnamon. In a separate medium-sized bowl, combine the eggs, sugar, vegetable oil, apples and carrots. Add the egg mixture to the dry ingredients and stir well. Line two standard 12-cup muffin tins with paper liners.

KIDS 6 and up: Divide the batter evenly among prepared muffin cups, filling each one about three-quarters full.

ADULTS: Bake the muffins for 20-25 minutes. When a toothpick comes out clean from 1 or 2 of the muffins in the center of the pan, remove them from the oven. Cool the muffins for at least 1 hour before frosting them with **Classic Cream Cheese Frosting (page 118)** or serve them plain.

Kids Tips

- Leave the carrot grating to the bigger kids (age 8 and up) since it can be tricky for the small kids.

- Kids as young as 2 years old can master how to break an egg. **See page 8** for instructions on how to teach **Breaking an Egg.**

Cooking Tips

- Gala or McIntosh apples are good for baking.

- If you're preparing these for a large gathering, I recommend making mini-muffins so that you can serve more people. Remember to reduce the baking time to 15-18 minutes, since they bake faster than the regular-sized ones.

Photo by Trevor Frydenlund

Classic Cream Cheese Frosting

Prep time: 10 minutes
Total time: 10 minutes
Yields: 2½ cups

Ingredients

Two 8-ounce packages cream cheese,
softened

¼ **cup whole milk**

2 teaspoons vanilla extract

1¼ **cup confectioner's sugar**

Optional: **zest of ½ an orange** (about 1 teaspoon)

The first time I made frosting by myself, I accidentally used granulated sugar instead of confectioner's sugar, which turned it into a grainy mess! I've made frosting a few times since then and prefer using cream cheese instead of butter. It's a lot lighter than a traditional buttercream and kids don't notice the difference.

Directions

KIDS with ADULT: In the bowl of an electric mixer fitted with the paddle attachment, beat the cream cheese on medium speed until light and fluffy. In a measuring cup, stir the vanilla extract with the milk. With the electric mixer on the lowest setting, alternate between adding small amounts of sugar and a little milk until the frosting is thick and creamy. Scrape down the sides of the bowl as needed.

If the frosting becomes too thick, thin it with a little milk. If it's too thin, add more sugar to thicken it. If you're not sure if it is the correct consistency, try frosting something to test it out. Add the orange zest, if using, and blend for 1 minute. The frosting can be refrigerated for up to 5 days in a sealed container or frozen for up to 6 months.

Kids Tips

- Most kids love zesting the orange, shaking in the sugar, and pouring in the milk.

Cooking Tips

- To create zest, simply grate the orange peel with a microplane zester or grater. To change it up, use lemon peel for a different flavor.

- Make sure you add only a little liquid at a time because even the smallest amount quickly creates a thinner consistency!

- If you don't want to use whole milk, it's best to substitute 2% rather than use 1% or skim.

- When you're preparing this recipe for the **Oatmeal Sandwich Cookies (page 120)**, you can omit the orange zest.

Oatmeal Sandwich Cookies

Prep time: 25 minutes
Total time: 45 minutes
Yields: 3 dozen cookies

Ingredients

1 cup unsalted butter, softened (2 sticks)

1 cup granulated sugar

1 cup brown sugar, packed

1 teaspoon vanilla extract

2 eggs

2 cups unbleached all-purpose flour

1½ cup old-fashioned or quick-cooking rolled oats

1 teaspoon baking powder

1 teaspoon baking soda

1 teaspoon sea salt

1 cup chocolate chips (or raisins)

Classic Cream Cheese Frosting (see page 118)

This is the best oatmeal chocolate chip cookie recipe – period. No matter how distracted I am in the kitchen, they always turn out delicious. If they cook too long, they are dark and crispy, and when slightly undercooked, they are heavenly and melt in your mouth. Add cream cheese frosting to create sandwich cookies and your kids will be begging to make them every weekend.

Directions

ADULTS: Preheat the oven to 375°F.

KIDS with ADULT: In the bowl of an electric mixer fitted with the paddle attachment, beat the butter and granulated sugar on medium speed until light and fluffy. Add the brown sugar and blend for 1-2 minutes. Add the vanilla extract and eggs, mixing well to combine. Scrape down the sides of the bowl as needed.

In a separate bowl, combine the flour, oats, baking powder, baking soda, and salt and stir. Gradually add the dry ingredients while the mixer is on the lowest setting. Briefly mix in the chocolate chips or fold them in by hand.

KIDS 6 and up: With greased hands or two spoons, shape the dough into very small balls (about 2-inches in diameter) and drop them onto a greased baking sheet (or one lined with parchment paper). Make sure to leave plenty of space between each cookie because they will spread.

ADULTS: Bake the cookies for 8-10 minutes or until golden brown. Allow them to cool for at least 1 hour before scooping a small amount of frosting onto the back of one cookie and adding a second cookie to create a sandwich.

Kids Tips

- For kids just starting out in the kitchen, this is the perfect first recipe to prepare with them. It's easy, fun and will create a positive impression of helping in the kitchen.

- Kids as young as 2 years old can master how to break an egg. **See page 8** for instructions on how to teach **Breaking an Egg.**

Cooking Tips

- If you don't have a standing electric mixer, it's possible to prepare these cookies by hand (or using a hand mixer). Just leave the butter at room temperature so it's softened or microwave it for just a few seconds so that the butter remains solid but very soft. You cannot use melted butter in this recipe.

Recipe adapted from Martha Vineyard's Black Dog Café, used with permission from The Black Dog Bakery, Martha's Vineyard, MA.

Quick-n-Easy Brownies

Prep time: 20 minutes
Total time: 50 minutes
Yields: 16-20 brownies

Ingredients

2 teaspoons butter or cooking spray

4 ounces Baker's unsweetened chocolate

1 cup unsalted butter (2 sticks)

1½ cups granulated sugar

3 large eggs

2 teaspoons vanilla extract

½ teaspoon sea salt

1 cup flour

This recipe is chocolate heaven! It can be made quickly and doesn't require a double-boiler for the chocolate. Brownies often dry out quickly so be sure to store them in a sealed container as soon as they cool down.

Directions

ADULTS: Preheat the oven to 350°F.

KIDS 6 and up: Grease a 8-inch by 8-inch baking pan with butter or cooking spray.

ADULTS: In a medium-sized saucepan, melt the chocolate, butter, and sugar over low heat, stirring constantly until melted. Keep a close eye on the chocolate to make sure that it doesn't burn. (Alternatively, you can microwave the chocolate, butter and sugar in a microwave-safe bowl in 30-second intervals until it is melted.) Let the chocolate mixture cool to room temperature – about 10-12 minutes.

KIDS 6 and up: In a small bowl, beat the eggs until light and foamy. Add them to the chocolate mixture, stirring constantly until it is well combined. Stir in the vanilla extract and salt. Gradually add the flour, stirring until completely incorporated. Pour the batter into the prepared pan.

ADULTS: Bake the brownies for 30-35 minutes or until a toothpick inserted into the center comes out clean. Allow the brownies to cool before cutting them into squares. Store brownies in an airtight container for 1-2 days at room temperature or freeze them for up to 2-3 months.

Kids Tips

- The kids can break up the chocolate squares, crack and beat the eggs, and measure all the ingredients.

- Kids as young as 2 years old can master how to break an egg – they actually pick up the skill very quickly! **See page 8** for instructions on how to teach **Breaking an Egg.**

Cooking Tips

- You can use any high-quality baking chocolate in place of Baker's chocolate.

- Make sure that the chocolate mixture is cooled down to room temperature before adding the eggs so that they don't scramble.

- If you prefer your brownies sweeter, add an extra ½ cup of granulated sugar to the batter. For chocolate lovers, add 1 cup of semi-sweet chocolate chips on top of the brownies before putting them in the oven.

Recipe adapted from Marlyn Grossman

Caramelized Bananas
with Vanilla Ice Cream

Prep time: 10 minutes
Total time: 15 minutes
Serves: 3-4

G
Free

Ingredients

3 medium-sized firm bananas, peeled

2 tablespoons unsalted butter

2 tablespoons brown sugar, packed

2 tablespoons orange juice

⅛ teaspoon ground cinnamon

⅛ teaspoon ground nutmeg

1 pint of vanilla ice cream

Optional toppings: **chocolate chips, peanut butter chips, or sprinkles**

This recipe looks like a gourmet dessert from a fancy restaurant – yet you can whip it together in minutes using standard ingredients found in most households. My students, both big and small, sigh with pleasure when they take their first blissful bite of this dish.

Directions

KIDS 4 and up: Carefully cut the bananas in half and lengthwise.

ADULTS: Melt the butter in a non-stick skillet over medium heat. Add 1 tablespoon of brown sugar and lay the bananas slices on top, cut side up. Cook for just 2-3 minutes and add the orange juice and sprinkle in the cinnamon and nutmeg. Cook them for 1 more minute, then gently flip the bananas over, and sprinkle the other tablespoon of brown sugar over the top. Cook them for 2-3 more minutes and remove from heat.

KIDS 4 and up: Serve the bananas with a scoop of vanilla ice cream and drizzle the leftover pan-sauce over the top. Garnish with optional toppings and serve immediately. This dish does not store well.

Kids Tips

- Since the majority of this recipe takes place at the stove, encourage kids to come up with creative garnishes.

- If you have whole nutmeg in the house, kids can use a microplane zester to grate it.

- Get creative and make Caramelized Banana Splits or have the kids come up with their own banana desserts!

Cooking Tips

- Make sure that the bananas you use for this recipe are not too ripe and that you don't cook them for too long or they will become mushy and fall apart. The ideal banana is yellow with a little bit of green at the top.

Index